Breakfast
in the
Bathtub

A Book of Smiles

Poems, short tales, vignettes, mini-essays...
whatever it takes

Fred Samuels and Joann Snow Duncanson

For Nancy —
Hope you enjoy
our book!

Joann Snow Duncanson

Peter E. Randall Publisher
Portsmouth, NH 2005

Peter E. Randall Publisher
Box 4726, Portsmouth, NH 03802-4726

ISBN: 1-931807-41-8

Library of Congress Catalogue Conrol Number: 2005906999

Other relevant books by these authors:

Who Gets the Yellow Bananas?
> by Joann Snow Duncanson, Peter E. Randall Publisher
> 2000

To Spade the Earth (Poems)
> by Frederick Samuels, Free Flow Press 1999

Intense Experience: Social Psychology Through Poetry
> by Frederick Samuels, Oyster River Press 1990

Human Needs and Behaviors
> by Frederick Samuels, Schenkman Publishing
> Company, Inc. 1984

Cover illustration and all artwork by Bob Nilson

PREFACE

GRATITUDE
in memory of Joann Lipshires

And now she's gone
as all must do.
Oh how she made us smile!

— F. S., June 2004

We hope that when we are gone, someone will write that we made people smile.

In this grim, benighted world of frightened and frightening mortals, there certainly is a multitude of non-smiling poems and essays to write. And there is need for these. However, there is perhaps an even greater need for humor in order to keep a healthy perspective on life—and to keep *us* healthy and more able to deal with whatever may confront us.

F. S. and J. S. D.
July 2005

ACKNOWLEDGMENTS

The following poems by Fred first appeared in *The Poet's Touchstone* (Journal of the Poetry Society of New Hampshire):
Community, Honey, The Ragatoo, After I Pass, and an earlier version of The Funnybone Blues.

The following poems by Fred first appeared in *Intense Experience: Social Psychology through Poetry*, published by Oyster River Press:
To Those Who Injure Trees, Gestalt, and Unconscious.

All of Joann's essays first appeared in *The Peterborough Transcript*.

Her poem, Rolling Home, first appeared in *The Poet's Touchstone*.

To all those who have inspired me to recognize and embrace joy when I see it, and then to pass it on.

J. S. D.,   July 2005

To those who can laugh at themselves.

F. S.,   July 2005

A Conversation
Fred & Joann

FS: Joann, what does humor mean to you?

JSD: Humor means almost everything to me—it's one of the best gifts in life I ever received. I like to think that my sense of humor came to me by way of my Aunt Gert, who was born with more than her share of funny bones. No matter how bad things got, she could always find something to laugh about, and so it's been with me. These days when I hear people trying to decide what to include in a healthful diet, my answer to them is simple: put a little humor on the menu. Not only will it make you feel good, it won't promote weight gain!

JSD: Fred, what made you decide that this book should center on humor—making people smile?

FS: I guess that I can claim that humor "is in my blood." That is, after all, one of many Jewish stereotypes. In the ghettos and *shtetls* of Europe, the Jews *needed* humor for survival. Pogroms—which were usually peasants taking out their economic subjugation and frustration on the Jews in the form of beating and plundering—were, you see, really a means of improving the species. Those Jews who survived were probably faster runners, or more accomplished hiders, or—in some cases, thank God!—better counterpunchers. Thank you peasants and oppressive war lords!

And with all that, a good sense of humor was indispensable to mental balance. And how long would survival last without mental balance?! Better to laugh than to cry. And it is still so for all of us—of whatever group. So I want to leave something of value. I have joined with the *Yellow Bananas* lady and we have got us a funny book! I always like to see happy people. Happy people do not make pogroms.

FS: What do you look for when you seek material for your humorous newspaper columns?

JSD: I look for people or situations that make me break into a smile, then hope that by writing about them I will cause my readers to smile as well. As you'll see by my story, "Breakfast in the Bathtub," when I discovered that my friend Jacquie had this very strange morning ritual, I just had to write about it. Often I don't have to look any further than at my own foibles. For instance, the day I drove through the garage door without opening it first.

I often come upon humor in the midst of an otherwise serious situation. In my poem, "Hair Apparent," I take a lighthearted look at what it was like to lose my hair while on chemotherapy for breast cancer. Luckily, funny bones are not always wiped out by harsh treatment chemicals!

In short, I find humor where Erma Bombeck did—just about everywhere. Thank heavens!!

JSD: Fred, what about humor in the workplace? For instance, how were you able to utilize humor in your role as college professor?

FS: I did indeed use humor in my teaching. Social psychology, after all, deals with human interaction, and to contradict Lou Lehr, *humans* (not monkeys) are the craziest people. There is, of course, an underlying tragedy in being a human mortal, but within that awful context there is much humor in our behavior. And it is important and even necessary for us to see life in perspective if we are to be mentally healthy.

Certainly I did not use humor to put down my students: that would have been cruel and unusual punishment. And, alas, they put themselves down far too often. I would, on occasion, laugh at myself and at other "authorities" in academia for thinking that we knew so much. I always encouraged the students to think for themselves, incorporating anything of value that I might present, and to make paper airplanes from the rest of the notes and sail them out the window. Thankfully, they did not carry out the latter part of that advice—at least not through *my* classroom windows. I had enough on my hands dealing with the administration, thank you!

FS: Joann, who is the funniest person you know?

JSD: Funny people come in various packages. You, Fred, always amaze me with your capacity to be at home with weighty world issues, while managing to find humor in everyday nature—both human and four-or-more footed—as in your poem, "Spider In My Universe." My brother Sky, on the other hand, falls under the category of story teller; no matter what the situation is, he has a humorous story or anecdote to match it. My sister-in-law Jean is a punster—a master of the one-liners, and always fun to have around. But my vote for funniest person I know goes to my friend Jane, who is just plain zany.

I never appreciated her humor more than after my husband died of a heart attack and I was left with two young children to raise. Jane was a constant companion during what she refers to as my "fuzzy period." This, according to the books on grief, is a stage where we go out and try to replace what we lost by doing odd, uncharacteristic things. In my case, it was shopping, and Jane was always there riding shot-gun on those trips. I still recall the day we were passing through the appliance section of Sears when an eager young salesman approached us. Jane just walked up to him, raised her hand to stop him and said, "Forget it, mister, this woman has already bought everything you've got!" Could she have been referring to my new dishwasher, clothes dryer, sewing machine, and toaster oven?

Yes, Jane remains the funniest person I know, even if she does still ask me—30 years later—whether I've gotten over my "fuzzy period" yet! (I have included a poem about her in this book. Look for "Jane.")

JSD: Whose humor do you enjoy—in literature, films, or television?

FS: At this point I come up with an even half-dozen of my favorites: Jean Shepherd, Henry Morgan, Sid Ceasar, the Marx Brothers, Jonathan Winters, and Garrison Keillor. Half midwest and half east coast it would seem, a majority of essentially radio personalities.

Jean Shepherd, perhaps my first place choice, is the only one of these who actually read something of mine on the air. At the time he was sponsored by Volvo, so I sent him a light humorous ad which I composed touting that car as a sexy thing. He said, "I like this little poem by this guy in Brooklyn." Well, thanks Jean, but it is half a century now— and I still have not received a sexy, shiny gift from Volvo!

FS: Joann, do you think that our readers may have had enough of our respective humor backgrounds, and that they would like us to "get on with it?"

JSD: Definitely! It's time for them to get into our poems and stories. It's time to have them smile!

CONTENTS

YOUNG AT HEART

HONEY

The plump, young secretary
at the doctor's office
calls me "Honey" when I come
for my monthly shot
of "Johnny Walker red"
(B-12 to the unhip).

I smile as an old graybeard
is expected to do, but
a part of that smile eludes her
—for she does not know that
I still view all women
through the X-ray eyes of imagination.

FS

BREAKFAST IN THE BATHTUB

My friend Jacquie eats breakfast in her bathtub every morning. Now to some people that may seem a bit weird, but different strokes for different folks, I say. Anyway, she told me that one day she had just gotten all settled in her sudsy water when she accidentally knocked her cereal bowl and its contents right into the tub with her. "I just sat there looking at those blueberries, banana slices, and fruit loops floating in the bubbles," she said, "and I laughed!"

So you see, people who are inclined to have breakfast in their bathtubs don't get rattled easily. That's just one of the many traits that make offbeat people like Jacquie such fun to be around.

I have another friend Sue, who although a grown person, still has this thing about stickers—you know, the kind that fascinate little kids. When you get a letter or gift from her, you can be sure the thing is covered with stickers. She has so many of them that they are beginning to take over her entire house. When her physician husband confronted her one day about the encroaching stickers, she reminded him that she knew plenty of doctors' wives who spent their money on things that cost a whole lot more than stickers do. So much for that conversation.

Then there was Augusta, the artist friend of mine who decided to do battle with the Grim Reaper. In her eighties and pronounced terminal by the medical world, the end of her talented and productive life seemed precariously near. Hospice was called to her old New Hampshire farmhouse to provide care for her. Well, they cared and they cared and they cared but this feisty patient showed no signs of going anywhere.

One day during a visit I asked Augusta what she felt was responsible for her health reprieve. "That's simple," she snapped. "I owe a lot on this old place and I'm not going anywhere until I win the lottery and get it paid up!" She was convinced that it was in the cards for her to be a big winner. She wouldn't dream of missing a week of purchasing her tickets.

This went on for a year and a half or more. Finally one day she called and told me to come out to her studio and select any of her paintings I wanted; her hopes on winning the lottery were dwindling. It wasn't long after that day that her body could wait no longer—lottery or no lottery. Today, two beautiful floral paintings hang in my house as reminders of a woman not only with enormous talent, but who thought outside the box for as long as she could; a spunky woman who may not have realized her dream, but was determined to die trying.

The way I see it, people who shun the predictable and do things a little differently than we would—things that some people might even call downright kooky—can sometimes offer us a welcome departure from our own somewhat humdrum routines.

I'm reminded of this every time I run into a group of those Red Hat Ladies. These are the fun-loving femmes who took their cue from Jenny Joseph's poem, "Warning," which began, "When I am an old woman I shall wear purple/With a red hat which doesn't go and doesn't suit me." Last month I spied some of them at Connecticut's Foxwoods Casino, their red hats and purple dresses weaving happily through the crowd of serious gamblers. By contrast, these ladies were out for a good time, and they didn't care who knew it.

I saw a bumper sticker the other day which pretty much sums this all up. It read, "Well-behaved women rarely go down in history!" How true!

And my friend who eats breakfast in her bathtub? Well, you've got to admit that it's not everyone who can satisfy three daily food group requirements and pamper her body at the same time!

JSD

THE LADIES LOOK LOVELY ON FRIDAYS

The ladies look lovely on Fridays—
rare beauties, to anyone's gaze.
They've just had their hair coiffed at salons
and they *pray* it will last seven days.

It does fairly well through the weekend—
still lacquered and fashioned in place—
and the ladies go forth in their circles
with great reassurance and grace.

But by Monday, things start to unravel—
by Tuesday, more strands go astray—
they all start to panic on Wednesday
and fill up the air with hair spray!

By Thursday they're downright *unsightly*—
so ashamed that they hardly can speak—
but the next day, thank heavens, is Friday
when they're lovely again, *for a week!*

JSD

AT WALLIS SANDS

Young woman in black string bikini
flies red-yellow-green kite;
it dives, rises, dances, dances,
its white tail wiggles, wiggles in wind
as she walks the clean sands of May.

FS

WINNIPESAUKEE*

Ellacoya—warm, shallow waters
where aging muscles loosen
to imitate frog and dolphin
as children frolic
in the Smile.

---

* *Lake Winnipesaukee, the Indian name translatable as "smile of the great spirit." Ellacoya State Park is on the lake.*

FS

II

KIDS

WATCHING HANNAH GROW

It was about eight years ago when we first laid eyes on Hannah. She was bundled up in a baby carriage, being pushed along our condominium drive by her mother. We were the owners of the condominiums—they were the neighbors in the house just across the road.

With no carriage-friendly sidewalks in the area, our safe drive, with its gardened circle down at the end, seemed a perfect place for little Hannah to be walked.

Most of us were in or near the grandparent age: young enough to remember the joys children bring, yet old enough to luxuriate in the knowledge that we could enjoy them without all that heavy parental responsibility. So when Hannah's rides along our driveway became more frequent, we settled in for what was to become a very welcome ritual, kindling memories of our own baby and carriage days.

Hannah eventually graduated to a stroller, and then before we knew it, she was learning to ride a tricycle. Her movements were tentative at first, this was a wisely cautious child. Steadily but surely, under the guidance of her mother, she passed the point of no return as far as self sufficiency on three wheels was concerned. She was beginning to taste a little freedom as she maneuvered, ever so slowly, around the circle.

It wasn't long before that tricycle turned into a training bike. Almost every day she would be wheeling through on that bigger, higher bike, occasionally listing to one side or the other, with those extra two wheels squeaking and teetering along for balance.

Then, of course, the inevitable happened: the training wheels were gone and Hannah proudly began to master the art of balance, zig-zagging along the drive with her father in close pursuit. Fathers often get called upon when children graduate to two wheelers—that's one of the many things in which they are expected to excel. Gradually Hannah, helmet on head and eyes trained straight ahead, rode faster and faster, while we, her grandmotherly and grandfatherly audience, would hold our collective breath for fear that in her exuberance she would lose control and fall before our very eyes.

While visiting during summer vacations, my own grandchildren have ridden their bikes around that same circle. More bold and daring than Hannah, they would wheel up and down the various driveways and race each other around the circle with such abandon that I hardly dared to watch.

Hannah has always been much more cautious. Whenever one of us drives in, for instance, she pulls over to the side and comes to a complete halt until we have gone by. She does this either because she knows many of us are aging and might forget where we are supposed to be driving, or she is the product of parents two have taught her well; I suspect it is a combination of the two.

These days, a flash of color outside my window often catches my eye. I will look out and sure enough, there is Hannah in her hot pink helmet, zipping around on a sky blue bike, maneuvering that circle with great speed and matching self assurance.

A sobering thought came to me recently. The way time flies, it won't be long before this delightful neighbor girl will be fully launched; she will progress to middle school, high school, be dating boys and yes—driving a car! We have to face the fact that when this happens, our condominium driveway will no long serve as Hannah's proving ground. I don't suppose she has the slightest idea of the lift to the spirit her drive-throughs deliver to some of us onlookers. In a way, that's the best part.

For now, I don't intend to dwell on the fact that she'll someday outgrow us. I'm just going to continue to enjoy occasional glimpses of girl and bike whipping around that circle with great abandon and speed. In other words, I plan to savor what's left of watching Hannah grow.

JSD

14 Breakfast in the Bathtub

KIDS' STUFF

When my granddaughter Hope was six years old, she collected band-aids. Not clean, just-out-of-the-box band-aids, but USED band-aids. The kind that have already been on someone's elbow, knee, or other place where blood's been drawn and scars now reside.

Hope didn't gather up these band-aids and stash them away in a drawer; she affixed them to the door of her bedroom for all to see. I don't know why, and I was afraid to ask. It had been a long time since I was her age, and if I inquired "why" too many times, that gap in our ages would seem like the Grand Canyon. So I told her that it was a wonderful collection, all the while hoping I wouldn't get a cut or scrape, or she might be dogging me for my used bandages. I figured she'd probably already set her course in life as an Emergency Room Doctor.

There was one other interesting item on her bedroom door—a handmade cardboard affair that she said was the equivalent of a scanner, and anyone who wanted to enter her room needed to have a special bar code, much like the ones on items you buy in the supermarket. Her mom, dad, and brother all had their own (handmade) distinct bar codes. I did not have one yet, but she granted me special dispensation and allowed me into her room until, I suppose, she would come up with my very own keys to the kingdom—a grandmother's bar code.

This is a very interesting and delightful girl; "project" has become her middle name. Her hands and mind are flying from morning to night. Papers, stickers, scissors, colored markers, used envelopes—you name it and she's doing something uniquely creative with it.

Her older brother Andrew sometimes humors her and sometimes considers her to be what most big brothers call little sisters—a pest. I suppose this is a normal, universal reaction for a kid who finds himself sharing a house with a creature who has shorter arms, legs, and attention spans than he has.

To this day, in Hope's room and in more than one kitchen drawer in her house, are enough craft supplies to outfit an entire school. Whereas I remember being a child with only a few pieces of paper, a pencil, and one box of well-used Crayola crayons, many of today's kids are well fortified with things to work with. All this coupled with zillions of computer games and TV shows should assure them of never having to whine, "I'm bored!" (Well, almost never).

People of my generation are often decrying the fact that kids today have so many things occupying their waking hours that they never have time to be creative. "They won't know how to use their imaginations!" they whimper. Well wait just a minute now. How about Hope's used band-aid collection and the homemade scanner thing—don't tell me that's not imaginative.

One morning, after having spent an overnight at their house, I watched the grandkids waiting for the school bus at the end of their drive. Andrew, now a seasoned rider, took it in stride—bulging backpack and black trumpet case lined up on the pavement, ready for the fifth grade drill. For Hope, a first grader, this school bus routine was new, yet she skipped down the driveway, nonchalantly dropped her backpack next to her brother's and seemed full of self assurance.

Then and there I decided she was really ready for first grade—I just hoped that the first grade was ready for her! For instance, had her teacher thought to put a handmade scanner and bar codes on the classroom door? And heaven help her if she's wearing a band-aid!

JSD

LOVERS

At age seven I had the loveliest teacher a kid could wish: Mrs. Messenger. She was a tall and beautiful blonde, and above all, she was warm and caring to the shy, chubby, curly-haired boy that I was. I would have done anything for her. Heck, I loved her!

One early autumn day, on my way to school, I stopped to pick flowers from a vacant lot. They were gorgeous, golden flowers, even prettier than the roses in Mr. Rosetti's garden or the tulips in the Vanderzandens' front yard. I clutched them tenderly yet firmly in my sweaty, little hands and briskly walked on to school. I could hardly wait to see the smile on my beloved's face. Oh, what sweet anticipation! I didn't know then of Freud's theory of infantile sexuality, but now I know that he was right on!

I raced past Avenue J park and its serene poplars, turned left down East Thirty-Eighth Street toward the proper entrance to P.S. 119, still holding the flowers proudly. It wouldn't be long now, soon they would be hers. And then the moment this fat, little suitor was living for—her lovely perfumed presence.

"Mrs. Messenger, these are for you!"

I whipped the flowers from behind my back and thrust them upward toward her face, which turned as red as Mr. Rosetti's roses. Then she sneezed one mighty blast and gasped, "Goldenrod..!" Young Freddy had no knowledge of allergies; I had led such an innocent, naive life. She hurried down the hall while I stood there in dismay and distress. What had I done?! I had hurt the one I loved. The youngster could easily have been emotionally destroyed, but in a short while, Mrs. Messenger returned, *sans* bouquet. She smiled her wonderful smile, and I knew that all was well between teacher and super pupil.

I first imagined that she gave the goldenrod to some teacher she knew was not allergic—but then the devil in me began to think that it would be far more intriguing if she had given the accursed flowers to someone she knew *was* allergic. "Here, dear!" In any event, we never spoke of this incident and remained warm friends—but alas, lovers only in my dreams.

As for the goldenrod, we have long since been reconciled. Now, each time I see it along my woodland road or under my bedroom window, it reminds me of my beautiful, forgiving, golden teacher.

FS

HAY IS FOR WISHING

I was driving along the highway the other day when I noticed, just ahead of me, a truck filled with hay. Now, when we were growing up, we were taught that if we spied a wagon or truck filled with hay traveling down the road and we made a wish on it, the wish would surely come true.

But there was a catch to it. In order for the wish to come true, we could never look back at that hay again. Sort of a Farmer's Almanac version of the story of Lot's wife and the pillar of salt.

It was this never-looking-back-again business that presented me with a definite problem. The hay truck was traveling along directly in front of my car, so the chances of my never looking at it again were about nil.

But I had an even bigger concern. The hay on this truck was not just pitch-forked there, loose and wild as we used to see it. This hay was packed into those oblong bales—all squared off and precise.

Wait a minute, I said to myself, is wishing on these square blocks of hay the same as wishing on the loose kind? Would my wish come true, just the same?

While I pondered that, my mind began to replay my own history with hay. I grew up in the best of all worlds— right next door to a wonderful New Hampshire farm. This meant that I had all the privileges a youngster can have on a farm, without any of the chores. For me, it was a situation made in heaven.

The farmer and his wife were a wondrously happy couple except for one thing—they were never able to have children—so I became a substitute for the daughter they never had. I got to ride on the tractor and on the work horses, Molly and Dolly. I could climb up to the very top of the corn-filled silo, look down into the damp and compressed silage, and become absolutely giddy from its rising fermenting fumes.

And then of course, there was the hay. At haying time, I was allowed to ride back to the barn on each loaded wagon, without ever having to pitch any of it myself. There were none of these mechanically baled oblongs or round marshmallow-shaped hay bales then. This was the good old, helter-skelter variety—just the way God intended. For me, enduring a few scratches and pokes from spears of hay was a small price to pay for the thrill of that ride to the barn. And then, once the hay was in, I was allowed to play and dream up in the hayloft as long as I wanted. To this day, that unique toasty, dry smell of hay is indelibly etched in my mind.

Now I suppose with summer over, the farmers have about finished their last mowings for the year. Probably that truckful I saw going down the highway was a result of that. And this brings me back to my dilemma. Let's say I had made my wish on those geometric bales of hay the other day and let's say by some miracle, I managed never to look at the truck again—what do you think my chances would be of having my wish come true?

Call me a skeptic, but I'll bet you anything that even if that wish did come to fruition, it would probably come out square!

JSD

OF APPLES AND PUMPKINS

Recently I saw an excellent movie from China, *Hero*. As in the classic Japanese film, *Rashomon*, the use of different versions of the same event played a key role in the story. It just so happens that there is an event in my childhood which—in my own adult mind—is also entangled in multiple versions.

First, let us establish that I am an ethical man. Honesty. Integrity. Justice. As Gilbert and Sullivan might say: "I am the very model of a modern moral character." Or so I thought until certain childhood memories oozed up from my unconscious mind.

When I was six or seven or eight, I had a yellow, wooden wagon. I pulled it along happily and innocently enough until I fell into criminal ways. There was a small private hospital on the corner of Avenue J and Kingshighway in Brooklyn where I was born—and it had a lovely yard of apple trees. I recall pulling my wagon around the corner, walking through the driveway in back of the hospital, and starting to collect fallen apples. If there were not enough, I would take an apple and hurl it up into the tree—with Bob Feller ferocity—and more apples would drop to the ground and end up in my yellow wagon. I was vaguely aware of eyes watching me from shaded windows (no doubt admiring my high cut-fast-ball). I would then bring home the loot, carrying apples in my arms and pockets up the narrow stairs, and presenting them to my mother.

"Buster said it was okay," I lied. Buster was the chief administrator/owner of the hospital. We often had malted milks side by side in Kaplan's pharmacy, but we had never discussed the gathering of apples, fallen or otherwise. My mother knew me to be an upstanding young chap, and I imagine that she believed my lie.

Not far from the hospital yard there was a large vacant lot where I often found stray pumpkins growing amidst the weeds. They were so striking in color and size, so exciting. Nature was good to this roly-poly kid; nature was abundant. I must have believed then that the pumpkins just "got there" somehow. I was a kid of great faith—and naive. I didn't dwell on other possibilities—those pumpkins just "got there." This was not a conscious theft. Oh no. I was a good lad, so I would load a few pumpkins into my yellow, wooden accomplice and off I would roll to mother. Applesauce and applesauce cake were good—but pumpkin pie was even better! I was a happy hunter-gatherer.

At this late date, many decades afterward, I wonder more than I did in childhood about the perceptions of the people who watched me in the hospital yard and the few who may have noticed me emerge from the weeded lot. What did they see? A kid being a kid? A cute, chubby, curly-haired hoodlum? Or are both these images the very same?

And yet as I relate the above version, standard in my thoughts, other possibilities push into the picture. Perhaps I was really not all that daring, not all that villainous. I was just a good kid. Oh horrors! For although I am glad to be a moral adult, I am beginning to realize that I do not wish to have been a goody-goody kid. But alas, the true story may go something like this:

I pulled my wagon around to the driveway of the hospital. Buster had suggested that I do this, while we were sipping malted milks side-by-side on the stools in Kaplan's pharmacy. "We have lots of apples," he laughed. "You are, after all, one of our favorite babies." (He had been there six or so years before when I was born.) So I entered the yard and waved to all the patients looking through the windows. We were, after all, fellow patients of the Mayflower Hospital, albeit separated in time. "Hey, you'd better learn how to pitch!" shouted one old critic from an opened window as my tossed apple brought down not a single mate, again and again. And others derisively laughed with him. I hung my head in shame and tugged the half-loaded wagon home.

But there is yet another way that it happened in my mind. There was a strike on in the hospital kitchen. Buster then called up my mother for he knew of her reputation as a fine cook—and especially as a maker of applesauce and a baker of applesauce cake. (She never thought those apples were of pie quality.) "Freddy, Buster would like you to gather apples in the hospital yard and bring them to me." I took my yellow wagon and my toddler brother and between us we filled and refilled the wagon several times while the patients cheered us on, anticipating mom's applesauce delights that were soon to come. I was a local hero. Not a villain at all—not even just a selfish kid.

But wait! I still have an ace-in-the-hole to rescue my self-image as a daring young rogue: the pumpkins! Those exciting, enticing treasures! For beneath the surface of young Freddy's naiveté there was, alas, a suspicion—long suppressed—that some vacant-lot gardener had planted those pumpkins. Forbidden fruit!

Nearly seventy years later the truth is out. And the two Freddies, child and oldster, are finally reconciled.

FS

THE SEARCHING PARTY

There were four of us: Charlie was the oldest and the tallest, he was nine; I was next in age, eight; my brother Alan was five, as was his girlfriend Selma. We were The Searching Party.

We did most of our searching among the grassy traffic islands of Kingshighway, between Avenues J and K, in Brooklyn, New York. We were treasure hunters: lots of pennies, some of them Indian heads still circulating here and there in the 1930s; silver coins and nickels were often found at the bus stop; there was an occasional bracelet, ring, or earring on the ground; and there was an abundance of empty cigarette packs with their exciting silver paper, which we rolled into balls—but alas, none of our balls came out as neat as the exquisite silver balls which cousin Mel rolled.

The Searching Party was a democracy: we voted for our leader; first by individual voice vote. My brother voted for me. Perhaps it was payback for the day in Selma's backyard when that bully girl Harriet was pounding his toosh with a hefty wooden board each time his swing came back toward her. Or maybe he was just grateful to me for doing my big brotherly duty of protecting him from the bully boy Jackie, who seemed to find Alan irresistible prey. Then again, my brother's vote for me may have been meant as a bribe, hoping that in our next bedroom sock fight I would not throw the smelly socks at him with quite so much force. In any event I got his vote. His girlfriend Selma made it clear that she would vote for whomever Alan voted for—indeed would do whatever Alan wished her to do.

I voted for myself and Charlie voted for himself. Three to one: I was chosen leader. Charlie demanded a secret ballot, and I agreed. The outcome was the same. Ah, democracy! Fortunately for me there were no electronic voting machines in those days or I might not have won.

I would like to make one thing clear about our group: we were not just casual picker-uppers of pennies, etcetera—we were treasure hunters, adventurers, daring to cross Kingshighway. In our young opinions, we were not mere scavengers, we were vigilant hawks and eagles ever on the alert for our elusive prey We plotted and planned our excursions with great skill and precision. We were the proud Searching Party! Our *esprit de corps* was excellent and I ran a tight but just ship. Even today, looking back on it all, I like to think that I was the very model of a modern democratic leader—much like F.D.R.

Those were days when we didn't need expensive toys or equipment to enjoy ourselves; days when we had our own ingenuity and imaginations to transport us to all kinds of wondrous adventures. We had The Searching Party.

Those were wonderful times. Where have they gone?

FS

THE THREE KINGS

It happened way back in December of 1979, and unfortunately for one member of our family, I remember it as if it were yesterday.

It was Christmas Eve and my friends and I had taken our places in the sanctuary waiting for the annual pageant to begin. The church was alive with the usual pre-pageant chaos. Small people wearing miniature bed sheets were darting up and down the side aisles like so many celestial flibbertigibbets, their cardboard wings and halos flapping furiously in their wake.

Somewhat larger people, perhaps middle school age, were getting rigged out in adult-sized bathrobes, with ropes around their waists. Meanwhile, their high school counterparts were donning the more sophisticated offerings from the wardrobe closet—velvets, satins and jeweled crowns.

As I sat there waiting I thought about all the pageants which once fell to my late husband, one of the ministers, to organize and direct. It was never an easy task. Take the year that Joseph was chewing bubble gum, for example. His wife had just given birth there in the church chancel and he was standing close behind her striking a rather tender pose, when he suddenly blew a large bubble that affixed itself to the nearest object: the Virgin Mary's hair. For the rest of the pageant he stood there bending over his spouse, not out of admiration but because they were linked by a thick strand of Tutti Fruitti.

One year Mary had the hiccups and after a few minutes of this, the entire tableau turned into a mass of shaking shoulders and purple faces as kings and shepherds alike tried not to laugh out loud.

But this pageant, the 1979 version, was to be special because my son would be taking part. He and his friends Dave and Steve, all high school seniors, were to be the Three Kings. I thought how proud my husband would have been if he'd lived to see them taking part.

We knew that being in this pageant wasn't exactly a life-long goal of any of these boys; we'd heard rumors that they'd been hamming up their parts during rehearsals. But we mothers of the Three Kings (all sitting in a row and all named Joann) knew that tonight they would play their parts seriously. After all, not one of them had ever given us any trouble. Besides, it was Christmas Eve.

Finally the last of the fidgety angels had settled down, the lights dimmed, and the organist began to play, "It Came Upon a Midnight Clear," followed by Mary and Joseph pacing their way down the aisle. No bubble gum in sight—so far so good.

Then, with bathrobes tied securely and wings flapping, the shepherds and angels filed down the center and side aisles on their way to join the tableau.

Then came our song; "We Three Kings of Orient Are...." That was the signal. We three mothers straightened up in the pew, proudly waiting for our boys to come down the aisle.

I could hardly believe what happened next.

I turned to get a good look at the three kings and they were there all right, wearing the velvet drapes and carrying gold, frankincense, and myrrh. But instead of the jeweled crowns on their heads, they were wearing golf caps! And they weren't proceeding down the aisle in a regal manner, but were sauntering, almost to a jive beat.

I gasped. I couldn't believe my eyes. Giggles began to be heard throughout the sanctuary. Then, as if this weren't bad enough, as they'd pass their friends in the pews they'd stop and give a "high five" greeting, then saunter on.

I caught a glimpse of the minister in the next pew. He was fumbling for his glasses, to read the list of participants—obviously looking to see who was playing the Three Kings.

But this wasn't the worst part.

When they finally made it to the front of the church where they were supposed to kneel reverently, they did a little "hokey pokey" type dance movement, twirling one complete circle before they finally knelt with the others.

By then I had turned purple. If I didn't have such low

blood pressure I've have ruptured a vessel by that time. I sat on the edge of my seat, not unlike a rocket on a launch pad ready for lift off.

As soon as the strains of "Silent Night" began and the cast started filing out of the sanctuary, I jumped up out of my seat and ran up that side aisle so fast, I'm sure no Olympic sprinter could have made it off the starting line any faster.

I flew down the stairs to where all the cast members were still giggling as they shed their various costumes. The Three Kings, knowing full well that they'd just done something they probably shouldn't have, made a bee-line for what they thought was the sanctity of the men's room, but I ran right in there after them. They couldn't believe their eyes, but there I was, huffing and puffing and ready to explode.

"What did you think you were doing up there?" I asked. "I thought you would set an example for all the little ones here tonight...." When I finished my tirade the three boys found out in short order that hell hath no fury like the mother of a pageant king scorned. None of them had ever seen me get angry or raise my voice like this before, and suddenly what began as a joke didn't look so funny now.

It turned out that the most humorous part of the evening probably wasn't the Three Kings' antics at all, but rather the sight of one of their mothers running up the aisle and down into the men's room to reprimand them.

So that was the Christmas Pageant of 1979. The year that a fun-loving teenager's prank and a mother's sense of pride collided head on. As you can imagine, not a Christmas goes by in our house without someone saying, "Remember the Three Kings? Did you ever see Mom so mad in your life?" And we all laugh.

The last laugh may be yet to come, however. These infamous Three Kings are now parents themselves. Wouldn't it be ironic if one day their own offspring acted up in a church pageant?

I say, what goes around, comes around—even on Christmas Eve.

JSD

HOW TO BE A FOOTBALL HERO

The Brooklyn I grew up in, on whose streets I played stick ball and touch football, was in transition. There were still some horse-drawn wagons going by: for the most part the Borden's milk cart, the rag-picker's rambling contraption, and several local produce and fish vendors. The horses were big, hardworking, and clearly well-fed, for they left plenty of yellow-brown calling cards along the way, generally disposed of in short order by the city street-cleaning crews.

This was also a time when we still believed in the basic decency of politicians: they really cared about our welfare and they would not let harm come to us. It seemed a safe and friendly world.

This was the world of my youth.

I played a lot of touch football on East 42nd Street, between Avenues J and I, where my cousin Mel lived. There, I was known as "Mel's cousin." I was not called "Fred" or "Freddy," I was called "Mel's cousin." I got to play there as the youngest of the lot and, on top of that, from two blocks away, solely because I was Mel's cousin. He was the star athlete of the block: fast and personable. Me? I was still sporting my considerable baby fat—I was slow and socially challenged. But there were two momentous football events to come which would change that.

The first of these events occurred during a game of touch football—two-hand touch, to be precise. We played tough and the laying-on of hands was done with something more than religious fervor. As usual, I was the last one chosen and as usual, no one ever threw the ball my way. But I was playing!

I would go through the motions of trying to block out the opponents, of trying to tag them, and of getting "free" to receive a pass when we had the ball. My efforts, however, were ignored for I was of no importance in the eyes of the other players: too fat, too slow, too unproven.

And then came the fateful day. Big Jim from East 43rd Street (a rare but respected outsider) was our captain and passer. He looked and looked for a receiver; no one could get free—except for me. No one bothered to cover me for I was a non-entity. So Jim—in desperation—muttered a horrific curse and hurled the ball at me with all of his considerable might. It hit me in the upper chest and jaw as I grabbed it. My jaw was stinging, and I was actually seeing those prover- bial stars, but I held on for dear life. No, for *more* than that— for my chance to get respect, to be accepted as a player, a person who mattered! I held on and stumbled a few steps forward past the manhole cover. Touchdown!! There were looks of disbelief all over. The youngest, slowest, most awk- ward kid had held on to Big Jim's bullet pass.

Bit by bit I started to be guarded here and there, and now and then I'd receive another pass. But it took another event to really change my fortunes as a street athlete.

But before this second football event occurred, I must mention that there was a large change taking place in my life. I was shedding my baby fat, becoming a faster and faster runner. Well, to tell the truth, it happened quite suddenly.

At age eleven, one year ahead of the official age, I went to Boy Scout Camp. What a time I had! Homesick as Hell, but that was not what caused the sudden weight loss. I was in the Pathfinder tent, and to go to the latrine—which I did every night after lights out (perhaps extremely early onset of enlarged prostate)—I had to climb down a steep hill. When I arrived at the latrine there was a wondrous sight of luna moths and other insects swirling about the lights, so it was worth the trip.

After taking care of the other reason for the trip I had to climb back up to my tent, stumbling over rocks and roots on the way. It was quite a little hike, yet not in itself the cause of my weight loss. One morning, on a solitary hike through the woods I came upon some beautiful, white berries which for some crazy reason I felt I could safely eat. Some boy scout! I had eaten Poison Sumac berries, and spent the rest of the vacation in the infirmary, poisoned outside and inside and, of course, unable to eat. I survived and went home a leaner and wiser kid and have never been a fatty since.

So now we get back to touch football on my cousin Mel's street, only this time the new lean-mean Freddy was playing. I was getting my usual now-and-then attention when **it** happened. Going after a wide pass, I slipped on some horse manure still in the gutter, and fell right into it. Smeared all over with the stuff, I continued playing. I caught a very high pass; I caught a very low pass. Caught one to the left and one to the right. Jumping, leaping, sprawling, crawling, I caught every pass thrown anywhere near me.

After a while it seemed to me that my own passer was now testing me, trying to throw one that I could not catch. But still, I caught everything and since I could now run fast, I was scoring touchdowns again and again. I was not just a hero, I was perhaps the first Brooklyn athlete super hero—just prior to Jackie Robinson. I couldn't be stopped: it was a memorable day. Oh, the super hero status didn't last intact—but I was never again a non-factor. I was taken account of in every game, and once in a while I even got chosen next-to-last.

To this day when I chat with Mel on the phone, we inevitably recall that day. We speculate that maybe I was catching all those passes because no one wished to guard me that closely; to be too near that horse manure!

Perhaps. But we all know that horse shoes are lucky. Why not also horse shit?!

FS

AH, PEOPLE!

The following poem was inspired by Janet Jackson's Superbowl half-time performance—where more than her soul was bared—and the subsequent *brouhaha*.)

SANS APOLOGY

1.
This old coot at the poetry hoot
would sing a *rondelet*.

I'd sing it sweet as the harvest moon
a-tumbling through the sky,
and as neat as the swan who learns to croon
just before he'll die.

And all the guys and all the gals would dance
in naked splendor—*sans* apology.

(And then there was the Democrat primary
campaign.)

2.
And the naked dancers waved their arms
  upward
which seemed as prayer to some,
as blasphemy to others
who watched in awe and titillation
—these same folk who had watched
the jaded, cynical media
define the meaning of a scream.

FS

INFERNO

Old thin preacher
In a grey suit
Trying to save me
While the temperature hits 95;
Never sweating, never doubting,
Trying to save me,
Holding me up
From my cool pool.

FS

MY FIRST NUDE

There was a time in my life—high school through college and a few years beyond—when I thought that I might become an artist. I would be the new Paul Gaughin, working and living in Tahiti, bringing bold color and bolder images to the canvas, challenging the world with new visions and values, and experiencing the excitement of life as an artist. There was one problem: I could not draw, or, as they say in some art circles, I was a bummer as a draftsman. But that did not stop me from trying. My buddy, Justin, was a terrific artist, oil painting being his medium. I recall the time we went out sketching at the dumps in Canarsie, Brooklyn. My amateurish, primitive-expressionistic oil painting from a sketch which I did that day still resides in my attic along with a dozen or so of my other painting endeavors. But that is not what I brought you to this page to talk about. My first life drawing session, the first time that I drew from a nude model, is the topic *du jour.*

There was a special, extra-curricular, drawing club which met in the evening at City College of New York in one of the wonderful Gothic buildings off of Convent Avenue. Justin, who had switched from engineering to art, was a member of that club, and he had invited me as a guest to attend an evening session. I was then taking a daytime course in drawing, and I gladly paid the fee to attend the session. I had switched from engineering to chemistry to creative writing to sociology to psychology and then back to sociology—but, alas, I had not given up dreams of the artist's life. And—let's face it—if I was going to be Gaughin, I had better learn to draw nudes!

I had never seen a nude woman before, and I was sweating all over and barely controlling my excitement both all over and specifically, for I was a shy but "red-blooded" male. The model, young and pretty, and in her robe, looked us over, smiling, then went behind a screen and emerged naked. I tried to keep professionally calm like all of the art majors around me. Hell, this was just part of their job, drawing nude women. It was something more than that for me, of course; I shall never forget it. Each new pose which she presented found my fingers shaking and the 2B pencil struggling to render her feminine charms on paper.

The drawing course which I was currently taking was professored by Stuyvesant van Veen, he who had drawn the hand gestures for the famous study by the anthropologist Franz Boas who was comparing the gestures of ghettoized Jews with those of non-ghettoized Italians. Now some of you may be thinking that it should be pretty obvious that those Jews would generally gesture in a more constricted manner than would the Italians. Yes, but social scientists feel that they must prove an obvious fact with systematic research. I would not be surprised if someday a scientific study would inform us that obese kids ingest more jumbo soft drinks and jumbo popcorn portions than do skinny kids. You heard it here! Nor would it surprise me to someday come across a study suggesting that people having "van" in their name, are more likely than not of Dutch ancestry. Prof. van Veen was a good guy, patient with me; he encouraged me: "You have a natural distortion in your drawing," he said with a smile. "Not unlike a natural curve which certain bowlers have: it is not at all displeasing."

Well, it displeased me. Whether I was drawing three poles at the Canarsie Dump, a bowl of fruit, or a gorgeous nude model—I could not get on paper what I saw, what I so wanted to draw accurately. That evening, pose after pose was rendered by me in my "not-at-all-displeasing" way. I did somehow manage to render her excellent head and face neither remarkably well nor remarkably badly—but then the "curse" set in. Her slender arms were twisted by my "natural curve;" her sensuous neck was distorted into a zucchini look-alike; her tantalizing breasts came out as psychedelic strawberry ice cream cones—at least to my anxiety-ridden eyes. Her stomach was depicted as if it were a somewhat flattened version of the natural-curve bowling ball itself; her pelvis was a shadowy jungle of erotic, surrealistic shapes and textures.... All in all, my drawing was not a product I was proud to have manufactured. And then—at halftime, as it were—we all took a break and the model put on her robe and began wandering about the room to see what we had produced. Now I was seriously sweating. Would she see me as a *voyeur* with no artistic talent? That would have crushed my fragile ego. I worked feverishly on my last sketch, striving to develop a representation worthy of her lovely body. And then she was at my side. She studied the sketches in my drawing pad, then turned and looked into my eyes. "You are getting better and better," she said gently, then added more loudly, "It's nice to see someone doing my face." She flashed a smile and walked on to the next student.

As the years went by, I did eventually cast aside my dreams of the south Pacific, with me as the new Gaughin, for I could not overcome my own displeasure at not being able to draw it as I saw it. My love of color and composition could not compensate for my feeble draftsmanship in my own eyes. And, let's face it: I was unwilling to undergo the struggles and deprivations necessary to succeed in the real world of art. I did not have the fire in my belly! But I never forgot my first life drawing session nor the kindness of my first nude.

FS

ENVY

The girl just ahead of me in the mall coffee shop line
is tall,
beautiful,
and of no more than eighteen summers.

My eyes cannot help focusing on her back,
obstructed only by the saucy strings of her tomato-red halter top.
The landscape of her flesh is smooth and flawless.

My own flesh, once clear and smooth to his touch,
and every bit as perfect as hers,
has now become a canvas where the paintbrush of age
has daubed and splashed designs of ugly moles,
and the faint renderings of meandering blue veins.

Just when I find myself on the brink of drowning
in a swirling eddy of self pity and youth envy,
the young girl reaches for her coffee cup,
causing her tomato-red strings to shift ever so slightly.
Just enough to reveal—yes, I see them—
two small but determined brown moles, near the nape of her neck.

I catch myself smiling as I utter under my breath,
"There is a God!"

                                                              JSD

TOURISTS

Tourists are a curious sort—
We watch them through our towns cavort
With dangling cameras, eager faces,
Tee shirts touting other places.

Walking shoes on busy feet,
Trying out our every street;
Necks craning here, eyes peering there,
Partaking of our restaurant fare.

We envy them when they come here
To visit us this time each year
For while they marvel at big and small,
We hardly see these things at all.

JSD

JANE

My friend Jane is happier than she's ever been in her
whole life.
Never mind
earning the degree from a prestigious women's college.
Never mind
the year she traveled clear around the world.
Never mind
marrying Donald, the Harvard graduate.
Never mind
giving birth to two splendid daughters.
Never mind
graduating from Divinity School and
becoming a Woman of The Cloth.
Never mind
officiating at her daughters' weddings.
Never mind
becoming a grandmother.
Never mind
divorcing Donald.

Never mind
Never mind
Never mind
any of this that went before.

My friend Jane—
sixty-three years old and not counting—
nursing her arthritis between jaunts to Greece and Spain,
savoring an occasional Margarita in local bistro,
celebrating freedom in her Cape Cod house
in earshot of the yin and yang mantra of the Atlantic
says
she is happier than she's ever been in her whole life.

Carpe diem, sister!

JSD

CHARLIE'S LESSON

When someone pays me a compliment for something I've done and I begin to take myself too seriously, I have only to think of Charlie Spaulding and my ego plummets to earth in nothing flat. He was a great guy, and he certainly taught me a valuable lesson.

For years Charlie and his wife Grace ran a mom and pop corner grocery store/meat market in the Boston suburbs. Both gregarious people, they were known for dispensing hefty doses of philosophy along with the daily milk, bread, and tenderloins. He also was quite a musician; he played the violin and knew his composers as well as he knew those meat cuts.

The real love of Charlie's life, however, (besides Grace) was woodworking. He was a master cabinet maker. If it could be created in wood, he tackled it.

When our children were small, he endeared himself to them by giving them some of his turnings, bits of wood left when the lathe had done its work. Every so often our doorbell would ring and there would stand Charlie, grinning from ear to ear, holding yet another box filled with shapes just waiting to be transformed into little people, animals, or race cars. At our house, Charlie was the forerunner of Toys R Us.

When he and Grace retired they began to look around for something they could do together—something to fill a few of those hours they used to spend down at the store. They settled on picture puzzles, only they didn't just do a puzzle and crumple it up and dump it back in its box the way most of us do. Once a puzzle was finished they would affix it to a board with special lacquer and then Charlie would build a frame for it. Not just any old frame, by the way. He always made sure each one would enhance the scene it surrounded.

But Charlie and Grace didn't stop there. Their puzzles always depicted New England scenes, and when one was completed—frame and all—they packed it into the Ford wagon and headed out to that very spot. If there happened to be a church in the puzzle, they drove to that church and presented the minister with their gift. Often it was a farmhouse. We can only imagine the surprise when these folks opened their doors and found a smiling, grey-haired couple standing there holding a framed picture of their house.

Now I'm getting to the part where Charlie taught me a valuable lesson. It came toward the end of Charlie's life, and since he had such an impish sense of humor, I would judge that he wouldn't mind my sharing it here.

After Grace died, Charlie's health began to decline and he went into a nursing home. I couldn't get in to see him right away and I soon began to hear about it from his other friends. "Charlie is wondering why you haven't come in yet—he is so anxious to see you!" Finally I made a date for the overdue visit.

When I arrived, Charlie was at the front door waiting for me in his wheelchair. I was embarrassed to have been so late in visiting, but he greeted me with warm enthusiasm, saying how "absolutely thrilled" he was to see me. "Let's go down here where we can talk," said he, and I followed him down a long corridor to his room.

Once there, he again commenced to tell me how wonderful it was to see me, and I found myself beginning to feel like someone very important indeed. I must have made a gigantic impression on this man.

Then, in the midst of more exclamations of how momentous a day it was because I came, he excused himself to go into his bathroom. When he came back he said, "This sure is a red letter day! Hand me that calendar over there, will you?" I did. He quickly jotted something on the day's date, then passed it to me to place back on the wall.

By that time I was flattered beyond all logic, and couldn't resist a quick glance at the calendar to see what this dear man had written about my visit.

It said, "Bowel movement—small."

Charlie Spaulding had many talents, not the least of which was putting me in my place. If I had never met him, who knows how impossible to live with I'd be!

JSD

THE REAL SCOOP

Although I find it hard to believe it myself, this is a true story.

I pull off the Massachusetts highway at a dairy bar and go inside in search of something cold and tasty to jumpstart me for the rest of the ride home to New Hampshire. Once in line at the counter I'm studying the frozen yogurt flavors on the blackboard when a young ice cream disher-outer begrudgingly pulls herself away from chatting with her teenaged friends and shouts, "Next!" It's late afternoon and her hair and her apron look it. Not an easy job, but someone has to do it.

"One small cone of black raspberry, lowfat, frozen yogurt, please," I say.

The girl grabs a cone and hunches herself up and over the row of freezer compartments.

When she finds the black raspberry yogurt, she throws back the lid and starts digging. Then, scoop, pat, pack down—scoop, pat, pack down, scoop—

"That's enough, thanks!" I exclaim.

Again, scoop, pat, pack down...

"Excuse me," I repeat, "that's all I need."

"What do you mean?" says she, teetering half in and half out of the bin.

"That's all I want—so you won't have to scoop any more."

"But this isn't even the size of a Kiddie Kone," she exclaims.

"That's okay!" I reassure her. "That's all I want."

She repeats her bewilderment over the size. "But this just isn't a Kiddie Kone OR a Small!!"

"Okay," I venture, "just call it a Kiddie Kone then, but that's all I want."

"But I'm telling you," (now she's getting a bit huffy) "it's not as big as a Kiddie Kone!"

Still half hunched over the ice cream bins with scoop in hand, she is becoming more agitated. By this time the partially filled sugar cone is in danger of being squeezed to pieces.

"Listen," says she in an exasperated tone, "I can't sell you this cone."

"Why not?" I ask.

"Because it isn't a Kiddy Kone and it isn't a Small."

"Well," I reply, "please just call it one of those and I'll pay you for whatever you decide. I'm planning to pay the full price anyway."

"I'm sorry, ma'am, I can't do that." By now determined that she is dealing with a woman from Mars who has an aversion for standard size cones, she extricates herself from the freezer's grip and thrusts the cone at me. I can see by her facial expression that she can't wait to tell her fellow ice cream scoopers what a kook of a customer I am.

"Here! Take the cone! I can't charge you because it isn't a Kiddie or a Small!"

I stand there in amazement. What just happened here? She's insisting I can't pay, just because I want less than the standard amount. I wonder how many other people she let get by without paying for something.

I return to my car, with my "perfect for me" size cone, and I shake my head in disbelief. Is this ridiculous or what? I'm offering to pay for less than I'm entitled to and she won't take my money?

These days America's motto is: *SMALL is bad and BIG is good.* Drinks come in bottomless vats, one king sized burger could feed a family of three, and what movie goer in their right mind needs a popcorn container so big they can hardly wrap their arms around it? At the rate we're going, nobody's going to be able to wrap their arms around any of US!

In a couple of weeks I will be driving down by that dairy bar again. I think I'll stop in, and, maybe I'll order the Grilled Chicken Special, but without the fries and cole slaw. I can hear it now: "But the special comes *with* fries and cole slaw...."

JSD

LIBRARY ALERT

I want you to promise that you will never divulge to your local librarians what I am about to tell you. This is classified stuff that has to remain between you and me—or there could be dire repercussions for certain people—incarceration, even.

The other day I was on the phone discussing the problem of increasing memory loss with a friend, (who shall remain nameless because I don't want her to have to check into the Witness Protection Program should you squeal to a librarian.) We both admitted to sometimes misplacing the car keys, leaving our purses behind in restaurants and having increasing trouble coming up with names in a hurry.

I confessed that sometimes when I'm watching a TV movie, I get about half way through the thing before I realize I've seen it before. The older I get, the longer it takes me. I suspect that someday they'll be rolling the credits at the end of the picture before I remember the name of it and that I've seen it before.

"That's how I am with books," said my friend. (Here's the part I don't want you to tell your librarian.) "Time and again," she said, "I'd bring home a book from the library only to discover after reading half of it that I'd read it before. But I've solved that problem. Now when I check out a library book, I just look at page 39."

"What's page 39 got to do with anything?" I asked.

Then came the confession.

She says, "After I've finished reading a library book I open it to page 39, and with my pencil, fill in that little hole in the "9." This way, the next time I go to the library to pick out a book I can be sure I haven't read it already!"

Now having been a library trustee at one time, I felt my library police antenna beginning to quiver. Wasn't this tampering with someone else's property? Weren't we taught at a young age to take good care of our library books? Isn't there a *fine* for doing something like this?

While I am sure that she means no malice and assures me she is "very neat" about it—using a very light pencil—I can't help worrying that she may find herself being hunted down by some Library Association's SWAT Team some day.

I began to wonder what other library patrons think when they come upon these closed in "9"s. Wouldn't it be ironic if some of them got out their erasers and undid the dastardly deed, figuring they'd just tidy up a bit?

Actually, this may be just the tip of the book defacing iceberg. I know someone else with a similar habit. After she reads a library book she puts a "tiny dot" on a certain page before taking it back. Let's hope it's not page 39!

I feel a lot better now that I've gotten this weighty secret off my chest. Now we'll see how good *you* are at keeping from sharing this bit of news with your local librarian!!!

JSD

SMILE
for Penny, Beth, and Sang

From the shores of Lake Winnipesaukee,
"Smile of the Great Spirit," I come
down the Spaulding Turnpike to the circle,
across the bridge to Kittery, Maine
for my first encounter with therapist.
Warm hands sink into my flesh,
come at me from here and there
(I sneak a peek—no one else!):
caring, knowing hands loosen
knots of pain and worry; slender,
serious masseuse methodically roams
this old, tight body, explores
the sights with respect and grace.
I surrender my body, willingly,
graciously, I trust this woman.
I lie there open, warm, relaxed;
colors dance in my mind
to the drum beat, music
sinks into my soul; well-being,
peace, self-respect, strength; life
renewed, enlarged, softened.
The ninety-minute massage done,
I walk out as one big smile.

---

*Note: I have since found two excellent massage therapists in
Wolfeboro, NH, close to the "Smile of the Great Spirit."
A beautiful state!*

*We are, of course, speaking here of massage therapy, a highly-
respected alternative health practice.*

FS

OLD HABITS

It's curious,
            when you think of it
why men
            still on the sidewalk spit,
when their hair's been permed,
            eyes with contacts lensed,
and their bodies with musk soap
            so thoroughly cleansed.

Let's hope that we females
            in our liberation
never take up the habit
            of expectoration.

                                        JSD

THE FUNNYBONE BLUES*

A-rambling, wand'ring, wond'ring, I boldly
search
the world for funny things to have you smile.
Atop the clouds—for poets fly—I perch,
a-seeking, seeking, yearning all the while
to find the kernel, essence, magic of it all
and turn the frowns and scowls to happy faces,
to have the sad and dreary mem'ries fall,
the world abound in bright and joyous places.
At times I was so desperate I could cry:
so lost, so blue, "to-be-or-not-to-be;"
I felt so down and hopeless I could die—
until I looked in the mirror and what did I see?
Why the funniest thing in the world is me;
O Lord, the funniest fool on Earth is me!

---

*Thought you'd like to know: this poem is a "sprung-rhythm"
sonnet, a form championed by Gerard Manley Hopkins.

FS

IV

WHEN FOLKS GATHER

THE NIGHT THE LIGHTS WENT OUT
IN JAFFREY

I've heard of *dancing* in the dark, but *speaking to an audience* in the dark is something else again! When I was asked to be the August speaker at the Amos Fortune Forum in the Meeting House in Jaffrey Center, New Hampshire, I said, "Are you sure they want ME?" Not that I thought I wasn't up to the task; I've been out there addressing groups for over 25 years and I love the challenge. The problem was that during the Forum's 55 year history their list of speakers has been so impressive: economists, physicians, educators, government officials, anthropologists—noted personalities all. Now they were extending an invitation to the author of a book called *Who Gets the Yellow Bananas?* Hmmmmm.

After mulling it over for a week, I decided to accept— partly because I was honored, and partly because of the maple syrup. You see, no matter how grand the personalities who grace their stage, they all go away with the same remuneration tucked under their arm: a half gallon of New Hampshire maple syrup. How could I pass that up? Of course, I had no idea what was to befall on my big night.

While enjoying a pre-performance dinner at the home of a Forum host, we watched as a vigorous thunderstorm came through. There was lightning everywhere and it seemed very close. It wasn't until later that we realized how close. One of those lightning bolts found its way to a transformer outside the Jaffrey Center Meeting House and left the place in total darkness.

As I entered the hall, the last fading sliver of daylight was making its exit and I said to myself, *this ought to be interesting!* It may even rival the night I spoke at that men's lodge in a smoke filled hotel room in Manchester, or that memorable day I was playing my guitar and singing at a

Heifer Project farm while a gathering of nervous goats insisted on relieving themselves on my sandals. *But speaking in the dark*—this would be something else again.

Right away, the Forum committee people scurried around finding flashlights and candles to help us to not only see our notes at the podium, but to actually FIND the podium. They put a few low candles along the contours of the stage, ala footlights, and placed a tall taper on either side of the podium, in order to give the audience a clue as to where the speaker was.

Moderator Dan Leavitt got up to introduce me, and delivered the understatement of the evening, saying that this could be one of the most unusual nights the Forum had ever seen.

I sat there looking out at what I was quite sure was my audience. Here they are, I thought, fresh from dinner, the lights are out, and they have to listen to a speaker for an hour. I feared I was about to witness one of the largest group naps in history.

At the appointed time I took my place at the podium and said, "This is going to be fun!"

I then proceeded to deliver my talk, and was pleased to discover from the welcome laughter that the majority of my audience members were not in the arms of Morpheus.

Fifty minutes later when I concluded my remarks, vigorous applause broke out. I took it as a sign that (1) they were trying to wake themselves up, (2) kill mosquitos, or (3) express their approval of what had just gone on. At any rate, I was relieved to know they were still there and hadn't snuck out to go to a movie.

The night was summed up perfectly when at the candlelight reception following the program, a young man came up to me and in all honesty asked, "Were you the speaker?"

Some of us will never forget the night the lights went out in Jaffrey.

JSD

AUNT LOUISE'S GREEN MOLDED SALAD

Our family always looks forward to Thanksgiving Day, and this year's went off without a single hitch. It was splendid! I can't, however, say the same for Aunt Louise's green molded salad.

There were eighteen of us, spanning ages from 5 (precocious Carley) to 78 (Aunt Alice, who showed no signs of having had heart bypass surgery the week before). In between was an assemblage of fun-loving, fast-talking characters who make up the Duncanson clan.

We gathered ourselves around a table as long as half a football field and soon the serious business of passing an endless array of serving dishes commenced.

I braced myself for the complaints about the turnip. Every year a hue and cry goes out over this poor, maligned vegetable. "Oh boy," nephew Danny would say, "I can't wait until that makes it to my plate!" Or niece Linda: "Yum, yum! I've dreamed of this all year long!" We all laugh, knowing perfectly well that the chances of them actually eating turnip are as slim as their winning the lottery in a dozen states simultaneously.

Then suddenly they set their sights on another annual delicacy.

"Yuck! What is that stuff, anyway?"

"It's Aunt Louise's green molded salad."

"Moldy?"

"No, molded!"

Then a great long discussion ensued about how weird the salad was. Since poor Aunt Louise left this earth over twenty years ago, I felt it was my duty to defend her jellied pastel delicacy. I explained that in the '50s and '60s, these salads were all the rage. You would never think of serving guests dinner without having at least one Jello-based salad on the table. Often it was Aunt Louise's lime green variety, but sometimes you threw caution to the wind and switched to the lemon yellow version. At Christmastime you show-cased your culinary skills by putting together a three-layer beauty—green on the bottom, red on the top, and sour cream in the middle. There wasn't a cookbook published back then that didn't have a few of these salad recipes in it.

Even though I knew that this younger generation regarded these salads as outdated "retro" food that should have gone the way of Spam and fondues, I broke the news that they are still alive and well at many a church supper.

I couldn't resist asking these teasing, 30-ish, food critics to fast-forward to Thanksgiving 2022, and asked just what delicacies from *their* era they expected would still be on the table. No one came up with the slightest suggestion. I secretly scored a point for Aunt Louise.

After the Jello Salad 101 lecture was over, little Carley decided to try some of that green stuff. She put one spoon-ful to her lips and made a face. "It's all lumpy," said she.

"Yeah," cried all the nay-sayers, "what's in that stuff anyway?"

When they were told it was made of lime Jello, cottage cheese, pineapple, and a cupful of mayonnaise, I thought they'd split their sides laughing. There was no convincing this crowd after that. Aunt Louise's green salad was dead in the water.

But there was an upside to all of this. First, those of us at the table who happened to like this salad could have as much of it as we wanted, and second, we knew perfectly well that this salad was going to be back as part of our Thanksgiving celebration next year, and maybe for years to come.

And better yet—so, in a sense, will Aunt Louise.

JSD

OH, IT FLIES THROUGH THE AIR.....

My dad was famous among family and friends for two "magic" tricks. One of them was "the flying card." The first time I saw him do it was during a visit by our close friends, "Uncle" Louis Grossman, his good wife Sarah, and their children Millie and Morty, dear childhood friends whom I sorely miss to this day. They, mom, brother Alan, and myself were gathered around dad in our living room in our Avenue J apartment.

"It is well known that when people believe strongly enough and concentrate hard enough, surprising things can happen," said dad, as he held the deck before him in his large, agile hands.

"If you believe and concentrate, we can make a card *of your choice* fly through the air!"

We all listen intently to his soft, strong, and enticing voice. He turns to young Millie. "Choose a color, honey, black or red?"

"Red," she says.

"That leaves black. Now, clubs or spades?"

"Spades."

"Spades it is," beams dad.

"Ace through seven, or eight through king?"

"Ace through seven," says the bright-eyed ten-year old.

"Okay, ace through three, or four through seven?"

"Ace through three."

"Which leaves us four through seven," dad says calmly, and smiles.

"Four and five, or six and seven?"

"Six and seven, Uncle Jack!"

"Now, " he asks, "will it be six or seven?"

"Seven!" she shouts.

Dad locates the card in the deck, shows it to us, and then places it face down on top of the deck.

"Now it is up to you all to concentrate very hard and we will make the seven of spades leave this deck and fly through the air," he says, holding the deck dramatically before him. We all focus on the deck, hoping to see the card fly from it—even as I once watched the housetops to see Santa and his reindeer.

"There it goes!" he says, and his eyes move along the flight of the card. We follow his eyes but see nothing—except for Millie, who suddenly oohs and aahs: "I see it! I see it!" she screams.

"Will someone please go to the bookshelf over the couch and reach on top of that big orange book?"says dad, smiling.

Morty runs over, jumps on the couch and reaches on top of Ripley's *Believe It Or Not* from where he removes a card and turns it toward the group. Yes! It is the seven of spades! There are gasps and smiles all around.

"Jack," says Louis, his best friend, "may I look through the deck?"

Dad acts hesitant, then acquiesces. Louis looks carefully, goes through the whole deck again and then nods his head. "It is GONE!" And there is much puzzlement in his voice.

"You all made it happen through your concentration," says dad. "Thank you."

I saw dad do this trick many times since. There was always a demand for it. Some would request the flying card each visit, and every time the card was retrieved—whether it was from Zaida's hat or Aunt Leah's blouse, or wherever—there was a mixture of amazement and "knowing" smiles .

Yet to me, dad's greatest "magic" was his cigarettes and hats sleight-of-hand trick whereby he made cigarette butts disappear from under one hat and appear under another hat in the most exquisite and wondrous manner. His ex-prizefighter hands performed remarkably.

But this is not to demean the flying card phenomenon. Although I lost my belief in Santa Claus early and I never did believe in the Easter bunny, I still half-believed in the flying card for years—even after dad had explained the trick to me. Perhaps, like Millie—who continued to swear that she saw that card fly—some of us dearly wanted to believe in magic. In fact, we still do.

FS

COMMUNITY

"Man is gregarious!" proclaimed Mr. Pansegrau
in his thick German accent,
unopened umbrella across his desk
—ready to fight us off, or to intercept a ceiling leak.
And that is about all I recall
from his bumbling attempts to teach us
the complexities of human interaction
in introductory sociology a half-century past.

Since then I became a sociology professor,
and I hope that I taught something memorable
to the eager and to the slumbering.
At times I think back on Pansegrau's one line.
Surely it should be "Humans are gregarious!"
Oh how I'd "he/she, she/he"
—for I believe in full equality.
My one line: "We act on our perceptions,
and we each perceive the world uniquely."
Or this is how they'd remember me:
Prof Sam threw open the window wide,
breathed deep through nostrils, side by side
—like a bloody yogi!

Yet, alas, I have heavy faults as well:
I've been called "the unsociable sociologist."
Indeed I do enjoy solitude and independence
of action and thought—which carries social cost.
Still, more and more as the beard did grey
I came to enjoy the company of others;
I thrive on human touch and a genuine smile.

It takes some of us so long to awaken
—this argues well for a second life.

FS

V

PLAYING AROUND

UNCONSCIOUS

There was a Viennan named Freud
who filled an intellectual void:
"Suppression is no virtue:
What you don't know *will* hurt you!"

Have another Clerihew*:

GESTALT

"Now listen to this, boys and girls,"
said the eminent sage, Fritz Perls,
"The world is one oyster
—and you are its pearls!"

*A light form invented by a chap named Clerihew, consisting of
four lines with rhyme (generally aabb) and where the name of the
main character must be stated in the body of the poem; not to be
confused with the far-more-popular-five-line Limerick—or for
that matter, with the far-more-respectable-fourteen-line sonnet.
(Now, Fred....)

FS

And Whitman's ringing singing lines
burst loose the crouching soul.

FREEDOM
In response to certain critics.

Form and content,
content and form,
one fluid, one rigid
—that was the norm
in days of yore
before we poets grew free
to explore different genres
or no genre at all.
To communicate is the goal! (How droll!)
Where traditional form
aids the quest
—that is best.
Where variation breaks a "rule"
—that is "cool"
if it works.
Gerard Manley Hopkins
with sprung-rhythm sonnets
put sunlight in our bonnets;
T.S. Elliot's erratic rhymes
are for our times.
Meaning and beauty!
Not false rigid duty!
Let us not be sticklers
or worse, nit picklers.

FS

HUMOR

is healthful

better than grief

better than despair.

Humor is nothing to laugh at!

FS

JUST A DREAM, HEY!

Did you ever have a dream which made you smile, and yet—without any need of Freudian analysis—it irritated you as well? I had such a dream last night, and I'd like to share it with you because I'm hoping we can get a few smiles from this nocturnal episode.

In this dream, Joann and I were starting out on a walk with our son (I do not have a son—so let us call him "imaginary.") In this dream, Joann (not imaginary) says very forcefully, "No, I will *not* lock all the doors: I'm leaving some open!" The house, by the way, was a sprawling, gray, wooden house that looked to be of Victorian vintage, and it had *many* outside doors.

"But what good is locking any doors if you leave others unlocked?" I foolishly asked.

"Better to have some security than none!" she retorted.

I then replied as follows: "Okay, let me move all the valuables nearer to the unlocked doors, and let me put the keys in the car and clean out the trunk so that the thieves will have an easier time of it!"

"Now *that*," said Joann, " is silly!"

At this point I awoke with my cat Fury pussyfooting across my chest.

FS

AH, MUSIC

NHPR proclaims new goal,
they aim for more "information":
talk, no music, just talk, they say.
I balk at this abomination:
Oh lost balance, grim specialization!
Mr. Station Master, retract this disaster!
Music, dear sir, *is* information ...
... for the soul.

FS

AFTER I PASS

the bittersweet vines will finally
win the war, entangle house,
make it part of the Jungle.

The raccoons, fed by me for years
on the back porch, will tentatively
enter house and take up residence:
excellent neighbors for mice, red squirrels,
and bats—all long-time inhabitants.

I could make the deal even sweeter
by giving the land back to Native Americans:
An Indian casino will arise,
a New Hampshire Raccoonwoods,
and all the good folk can stay and play
here, and save the drive down to CT.,
thus cutting back on CO_2 pollution.
Yes, this will be my contribution.

FS

HAIR APPARENT

It sat upon my pate for years
so plentiful and fair
that friends would say "How fortunate
you've such a head of hair!"
I cut it, curled it, blew it dry
or combed it straight and stern—
I sometimes had bad hair days
that caused me much concern.

It went through changes color-wise
from blonde to brown, near black—
I sometimes piled it on my head
and some days pulled it back.
We went along for years like this,
my head of hair and I,
then chemotherapy barged in
and bade my hair goodbye.

It was so stressful on the day
my tresses split the scene.
I couldn't pull my hair out—
(not a strand left to be seen)
so I bought myself some wigs and scarves—
all sorts of subterfuge
to try to cover what was gone,
and I daubed my face with rouge.

And then one day, I touched my head
and what do you think was there?
A brand new crop of fuzzy stuff!
EUREKA! IT WAS HAIR!!
It didn't happen overnight—
with hair, it's such slow going—
but I kept peeking 'neath the wig
and there it was—still growing.

So, hair today—gone tomorrow?
That's just *half* the story,
for some of us get a *second chance*
to welcome our crown and glory!!

JSD

ROLLING HOME

From birth to death
we bobble along
on life's conveyor belt
like so many hapless confections
at the chocolate factory;

except
in our case,

there is no Lucille Ball
to catch us
at the end.

                                              JSD

POETRY IS THE HIGHEST FORM OF ART:

It speaks neatly, sweetly, indiscretely;
paints vivid images;
dances to savage rhythms;
sings from the guileless soul.
It can recall and contemplate,
be tragic, sad, or funny;
above all, it won't contaminate
by making too much money.

                                        FS

VI

CRITTERS

I AM THE VERY MODEL OF A MODERN
NATURAL GARDENER

There you go, Charlie Chuck,
    eating my peas
    as neat as you please.
My Have-A-Heart trap
    remains unsprung:
    and now I have
    to take out the gun.
It's time, Charlie Chuck
    to blow you away.
I swear I won't wear
    my Defenders-of-Wildlife T-shirt
    that day!!!

                    FS

FEEDER DAYS

The eagle, mighty beak and claws,
its high, majestic soaring,
earns itself symbolic place,
a populace adoring.

How many cheer the chickadee
who hovers near the feeder
when larger birds—grosbeak, jay—
have fled the human intruder?

The chickadees I see don't squabble
the way my other guests will do;
each chickadee seems ranked quite equal,
no hierarchic hullabaloo.

The band which graces my environs
are open-handed, if you please:
their ranks include a finch and nuthatch
among the gracious chickadees.

How cheerful are their morning greetings
as I approach with seed in beaker;
they sound like tenors and sopranos,
each talented and none a squeaker.

So quick they dart from branch to branch
I hear the music of their wings;
I've seen maneuvers in mid-air
which rival those of hummingbirds.

Let the majestic eagle soar!
My favorite warbler still will be
the operatic, aerostatic,
pantisocratic chickadee!!

FS

O THE SIMPLE PLEASURES

Fury Cat on the porch rail sits
a-watchin' Rockies eat.
The Rockies are raccoons, you see—
comical and sweet.
With their funny masks and tiny hands
they grab the kibbles and each one nibbles
as the feline observes in genuine awe—
they're the cutest "people" she ever saw.

And they watch her a-watchin' them
and she watches them watch her a-watchin' them
and they—you get the pic—
so I open the door and mighty quick
toss out dog biscuits to break the spell.
They pick them up and all ends well
as Fury jumps inside to eat her goodies
—a peace supreme in the critters' woods.
A peace supreme in the critters' woods.

FS

APRIL PURRRSPECTIVE

I am singing the old income tax blues
at the dining room/sun porch "desk."
Cat Fury jumps on,
heads across the papers.
I toss her off, gently—
she returns; more angrily
I push her away:
must concentrate on data, instructions.
I am into worksheet for figuring
how much of my Social Security
is eligible for government take-back.
Very involved.
Very boring.
I am sweating.
My brain cries out for freedom
from the convoluted calculations.
Fury is back on table,
her bushy tail swishes across numbers on page.
For some reason I smile,
then break out into laughter
as she rolls on table.
I tickle her tummy
and I laugh harder than I have all winter long.
I return in time to the tax
and continue laughing
at it,
at myself,
at all of us.

FS

SPIDER IN MY UNIVERSE

"It is after all a matter of perspective."
—anonymous social psychologist
"And who shall be judge of a creature's worth?"
—anonymous free-thinker

Shower on so furious.
Wait! What is that curious
black blob on the mat?
I stoop to examine that:
Spider—drenched from legs to head;
in a bad way (some would say, "dead.")
But I scarcely e'er give up on friends,
and this critter's life on me depends,
so leaning past the shower curtain
I place him/her on waste basket certain
that she/he (can *you* tell which one?)
is safe until my shower is done.

I carry arachnid to sunny sill
and place her/him where sun's heat will
dry the drowned thing, four front legs fused
together, body still, looking poorly used.
Now I blow air gently on soppy mess
—more desperate than cool, I must confess—
yet the body seems "alert" somehow;
to a sunnier window I place it now.
The sun soaks into soggy spider,
no shadow does hide him or hide her.
I return to bathroom, dry and dress,
back to sill in ten minutes or less,
and behold! The four fused legs are parted,
body still but poised: I am "uphearted;"
I leave again, expect the best;
when I return—you know the rest:
Spider's not there. He/she lives! Not odd.
It's a matter of care. It's such fun being God.

FS

VII

A BIT O' NONSENSE

THE RAGATOO

I
Under the tree
is a ragatoo
and he sits
with his feet
in the air;
his laugh is loud
and his smile is wide
and the hair
on his head
is on the inside
and he sits
with his hands
on a chair
that really
isn't there.
Oh listen to the chatter
of the ragatoo the ragatoo the ragatoo...

II
This ragatoo
is a friendly guy
who'd give you his shirt
or the back of his tie
or his otcoe hat
or his tidicoe scarf
or his satcoe mat
or this and that
—if it catches your eye.
Oh listen to the chatter
of the ragatoo the ragatoo the ragatoo...

III

The ragatoo's friends
come in every size
and color and shape
—and all are wise
for they live
in the land of Harmony
where all is love
and all is peace
and you don't hate
a guy because of his race
or the place he prays
if he prays at all
—that's his call.
Oh listen to the chatter
of the ragatoo the ragatoo the ragatoo...

IV

I'm a rootin' tootin' ragatoo
—part Christian, Parsi, Moslem, Jew,
Taoist, Buddhist, Sikh, Hindu;
I'm brown as the earth,
white as the clouds,
black as the night
with its radiant stars,
I'm bronze and red, yellow and gold,
I live in the hills
in the woods
by the sea
in the teeming screaming city streets,
I'm young I'm old
I'm woman man
I'm a ragatoo
that's what I am.
Oh listen to the chatter
of the ragatoo the ragatoo the ragatoo...

FS

REBUILT NURSERY RHYMES

Mistress Mary, contemporary,
How does your wardrobe grow?
With American Express and Visa
And Mastercard, all in a row!

Modern Miss Muffet
Sat on a tuffet
Downing her yogurt and Perrier
When along came a spider
Who sat down beside her
So she soon got up off of her derrier!

Jack and Jill went up the hill
To purchase a new Mercedes—
But with *their* poor finances
They have as *much* chance as
An icicle freezing in Hades.

Jack Spratt would eat no fat
His wife would eat no lean—
Making him a vegetarian
And her a sight to be seen!

Lean Cuisine hot—
Lean Cuisine cold
Lean Cuisine in the microwave
Two seconds old!

Three little kittens lost their mittens
And they feared their mother's sharp ire
Till she said, "Do not whine—
For the fault is all mine—
I shrank them to bits in the dryer!"

JSD

LET THERE BE LAUGHTER*

Through genetic deviation
or instant creation
or some alternative plan
the Lord made man.
When the light of the sun
revealed what He'd done,
He was amazed at what He had wrought:
not quite what He'd thought!

"What a disaster!
Can't he run faster?
        (Hell, he's no gazelle!)
And couldn't he be stronger
        (No ant or elephant!)
Or persevere longer?
        (This mammal ain't a camel!)
All he can do well is speak.
Oy! What a week!

Now it's time to retire,
but first he'll require
something really worthwhile,
a reason to smile.
So now I hereby decree
(remember you heard this from Me)
for now and ever after
let there be laughter!

(Folks, there may be a slight delay
 but the brothers Marx are on the way.)"

---

*This poem was jointly composed by me
and my late wife, Carol Stonham Samuels.*

FS

TO THOSE WHO INJURE TREES
(Meant to be read with "tongue in cheek.")

The ancient Germans worshiped trees;
they had a custom aimed to please
        the spirit of a vegetable
when injured by a ne'er-do-well:
they'd cut the navel from the culprit
and to the tree they'd fasten it
upon the spot where bark was peeled
where knife or axe the wretch did wield.
Then round the tree they'd lead the fiend
        until his guts wound round the wound
thus bringing life to life destroyed.
(Arbicide was a crime to avoid!)

Take heed polluters of today
whose smokestacks turn the green to grey:
if Osiris doesn't get you first,
the navel punishment may be the worst.

Note: The custom of the ancient Germans referred to above is described in Sir James G. Frazer's *The Golden Bough*, page 127 (Macmillan, 1963)

Humorous satire when used to make a point has its risks: years ago when I sent this poem into my round robin, one good person chided me for advocating such cruelty.

FS

CUR-and-PURR-SPECTIVES

A yellow Lab and a one-eyed cat,
companions of this poet,
will tease and taunt and this and that;
each tells the other: "Stow it!"

Such fun on hikes, this motley pair;
especially in the night time,
for bouncing along here and there:
two eyes, one eye in flashlight time.

When I go skiing in new snow,
dog Molly is trail-blazer;
I follow neat enough, although
cat Cathy follows like a laser.

Now Molly's growls sound somewhat fierce,
they certainly don't sound jolly;
her teeth the toughest bone can pierce;
I mutter, "Be a good dog, Molly!"

"That's an oxymoron," says the cat,
"The proofs are quite abundant."
"Quite the contrary," says Molly, "Drat!
'Be a good dog!' is redundant."

"Let lying dogs sleep," says Cathy Cat.

FS

VIII

STRANGE DOINGS

Emily Dickinson

GENESIS, REVISITED

And the Force created poets

—and there was Light!

FS

EMILY DICKINSON GOES TO THE MALL

I.

I was so surprised to see her
        standing at my door that day!
It's a hundred plus a score or so
        since they carried her away
in that little poet's coffin,
        through the garden, down the field—
they tucked her in securely,
        but she'd obviously come unsealed!

"Called back to earth," she blurted,
        "just temporarily!
Perhaps I've time to see a moor
        or look upon the sea?"
"Well, first things first, dear lady.
        Just look at you," I said.
"Your body is quite naked—
        not a stitch from toe to head!"

"But I have a dress," she whispered.
        "It's all in white, you know.
It goes with my simplicity,
        and father loves it so."
"You mean the dress up in your room?
        It's now in a glass case!"
"That sister Vinnie!" Emily chirped,
        "Always tidying up the place!"

She had, of course, no inkling
        that the dress, which once hung free
was being viewed by loving fans
        for a Homestead entrance fee.
But time was of the essence
        for this Maid of Metaphors
so I wrapped her in a raincoat
        and we headed for the stores!

II.
The ride in my Toyota
     had her frozen in her seat—
she looked in vain for carriages
     or Amherst's wide Main Street.
"Oh, do we go past Austin's?
     Should we stop to visit Sue?"
She said, "What about my garden?
     There's so much that I should do."

I managed to keep driving,
     but *believing this* was hard—
to think that 'neath that seatbelt
     sat a 19th century bard!!
I couldn't keep from smiling—
     we'll make history, after all
for today the Belle of Amherst
     was going to the Mall!!

III.
As we neared the entrance to the mall
     Emily's hand reached for my own.
She was frightened, and in her words,
     she felt "Zero at the bone!"
I tried to act quite confident,
     kept a sure and steady stride,
but if the parking lot's this scary,
     I thought, *wait till she's inside!*

In no time we were swallowed up
     by shoppers in a rush
and swept right through those big glass doors
     to a 21st century crush!
I wrapped my arm around her waist—
     she was looking pale and queasy.
Such a culture shock for her!
     This project won't be easy!

I'd pretty much decided on
        which store would fill our need
when suddenly Miss Emily
        began to pick up speed.
"I love the name Victoria!"
        she said. "May we shop there?"
But I somehow couldn't picture her
        in *their* scanty underwear!

                IV.
So I whisked her into Macy's,
        and as *she* would say in rhyme,
to dress her as "the sun rose,
        a ribbon at a time."
A pair of shoes, some underthings,
        so far we'd met success!
But the biggest challenge facing us
        was to choose a brand new dress!

I sent her to the dressing room
        with frocks of every kind
and it seemed to take a century
        to make up *this* poet's mind!
I thought for sure she'd choose the white
        but I was wrong. *Instead,*
she came out beaming ear to ear
        in a gorgeous dress of—RED!

One more surprise awaited her,
        and by far the greatest yet.
We were entering a bookstore—
        one she never would forget!
Her eyes grew big as saucers!
        On *all those books*—**HER** name!
No longer just a "nobody"
        but a woman of some fame!

V.

To all good things, there comes an end
      and so it was that day...
for as quickly as she came to me,
      so did she go away.
And though this happened long ago
      I always will recall
the day that Emily Dickinson
      went shopping at the mall!

JSD

MANY ARE COLD,
BUT FEW ARE FROZEN

If my kids are reading this, listen up!! I DO NOT NOW, NOR HAVE I EVER, WANTED TO BE FROZEN AFTER I DIE! For that matter, I'm not too keen on being frozen before I die either. I'm not a winter person, but I know that at least when spring comes, I can thaw out. I'm not so sure there'd be a spring in my future if I were to be relegated to the frozen section of some cryonic after-life supermarket. I don't imagine they bring birds and flowers into those repositories once a year just to boost our spirits.

The only positive aspect I could see about being frozen, is that I possibly could get to know Ted Williams, whose family has chosen this route for him. I never understood much about the world of baseball, but I always knew a good-looking man when I saw one, and he was definitely good-looking. If the Splendid Splinter and I got iced together, perhaps he could help while away the hours by transmitting some of his vast baseball knowledge to me—reading me some bedtime stats, reciting the names of Hall of Fame guys, or at least explaining that mystery of all mysteries— why baseball players have to spit all the time. Sure, baseball might not be the most interesting of topics for me, but a refrigerated hereafter could last a long time, and I don't suppose the library's bookmobile makes stops there.

Then there's that other matter—they say you are frozen in these cylinders upside down. That right there is reason enough for a person to beg off from being a cryonics customer. Granted, after you've died, I suppose that old problem of the blood rushing to your inverted head wouldn't be too big a factor. And speaking of heads, some folks are opting to have just that part of their body preserved. No thanks, I'd rather be in one piece, thank you. It's the whole enchilada or nothing. Of course, if I thought they could attach my head to Britney Spears' body someday, I might reconsider.

This whole business of cryonics is curious to most of us. I have many questions. For instance, are we fully dressed all that time? With a temperature of minus 320 degrees Fahrenheit, would a little polar fleece help, or since we'd be in liquid nitrogen, should we pack a wetsuit?

There seem to be two basic reasons for people to choose the cryonics route: (1) their ego is such that they feel their DNA alone will be worth something someday, or (2) they want to know what it would be like to "come back" to experience life in the far future. Personally, I can't imagine anyone clamoring for the DNA of a woman who helps make a living by writing stuff like this! And as far as coming back is concerned—I've already had plenty of blessings and challenges in this life, thank you.

The way I see it is this. Once you make up your mind that you don't want to go the traditional route—being lowered below the sod in one piece—you have two choices: fire or ice. Since I've just ruled out the ice route, fire seems the only choice left. For women, that may be a natural solution. Now that they've taken away our Hormone Replacement Therapy, what better way could we go out of this world than with one final, gigantic hot flash!

Too bad, in a way. Ted Williams and I just might have hit it off.

JSD

PUBLIC THOUGHTS ON A
PRIVATE MATTER

Today we are going to discuss the bladder. I know, you are thinking there are much weightier topics we could address, but believe me—when you reach a certain age there is nothing any weightier than the bladder.

The bladder comes into prominence during two periods of our lives—the beginning and the end. It is the alpha and omega of human organs. When we are infants, our whole world seems to revolve around the bladder—and the results thereof. The one thing we can always count on in a little bundle of joy is that he or she will produce a wet diaper for us. When my children were babies and cloth diapers were our only choice, I could have penned a sequel for Elizabeth Barrett Browning: "How do I love thee?/ Let me count the soaked diapers...." Now things are different. Babies still wet, but the awaiting diapers are of the very absorbent, disposable variety. Bladders can empty many times into these things before they need changing.

Something else in this department has changed too. In our family we referred to the wetting function as "tinkling." I know it wasn't too original, but that's all we and our suburban neighbors could come up with. Today's babies don't do anything as melodic as that. They pee. In fact, people of all ages seem to pee. I am still trying to get accustomed to the term—and the same goes for its companion term which is featured in the pre-school best seller, *Everyone Poops*, by Taro Gomi.

I do remember another brief time in my life when the bladder played a leading role—that was when I was in elementary school. Painfully shy, I would rather die than raise my hand and ask the teacher for permission to go to the bathroom. Instead, I squirmed and fidgeted through spelling lessons and math problems while the elasticity in my bladder endured the ultimate test. The final bell came none too soon for me—and if the school bus hit a bump on the way home, it was all over—literally.

For most of our lives, however, these bladders of ours recede into the background while doing their thing: they call, we respond; they call, we respond. No big deal.

When it does become a big deal, however, is when our age starts climbing over the speed limit mark. Suddenly the bladder and its appendages become very important. For women, it has to do with something Isaac Newton called gravity. Only instead of an apple that's falling, its the uterus, and it lands up against, and puts pressure on—you guessed it—the bladder!

This turn of events can change a woman's whole outlook and routine. A sudden sneeze or cough can become something of gigantic proportions. Also, there are things we used to do that we shouldn't do anymore. I found that out last summer while playing a game of volleyball with the grandchildren. I discovered that at this age, it isn't just arms and legs that leap and jounce during a game, the bladder does too! By the time the game was over, I was afraid I might have to sign myself in to the June Allyson School of Depends.

All this makes me think of the day last spring when a group of us women were having lunch and the subject of jumping rope arose. One by one we began to think back to when we were young and would join our girlfriends in this springtime ritual. We started to recall some of the sing-song chants we jumped to: "All in together girls/ Never mind the weather girls/ January, February....;" "Mother, Mother, I am sick/Send for the Doctor, quick, quick, quick...." etcetera. One by one we women began to say that we could probably still do a decent job at jumping rope. "Yeah, we could do it," we chorused. Suddenly, the senior member of the group, in her nineties, stopped laughing and a look of stark reality came over her face. "On second thought," she said, "you'd better count me out. When I was in my eighties I tried jumping rope—and my bladder fell out!"

I told you they were weighty. I rest my case.

JSD

HERE COMES THE GROOM—*VICTOR!*

I hadn't thought of Victor Mandorf in years, but recently something triggered my memories of the old neighborhood, and suddenly there he was.

The day he and his wife moved into the house next door all the neighbors were quite excited. We'd heard that newlyweds were coming, and since most of us were in our forties, with half-raised children, we looked forward to having some younger couples on our street. When they finally drove up behind the moving van, we discovered that they were indeed newlyweds, but the groom was in his late eighties and the bride in her seventies.

Suddenly I found myself living between two older, wiser, and seasoned couples, for on the other side of me lived Arthur and Peg Willis, eighty and seventy respectively. They'd just won the prize down at the senior center for having the most marriages between them—six! I sensed I was going to like this new arrangement and set about getting acquainted with the Mandorfs.

Virginia Mandorf was a well padded, rosy-cheeked woman with white hair, azure blue eyes, and the remnants of a Philadelphia accent. Widowed for years, she brought up her children on the small salary she made as "head of the coat department" at Gilchrist's Store. When she reached her early 70s, however, she tired of her work routine and began feeling sorry for herself. One day, on a whim, she answered a newspaper ad placed by a man from Wellesley who needed someone "to help with light housekeeping and cooking." She responded and the rest was history.

Many afternoons as I drove in from work, Virginia would call me saying, "Come on over, I'm going to hot the pot," which I gathered was Pennsylvania-ese for "make tea." Peg would be invited too, and I'd find myself with not just two delightful neighbors, but a pair of nurturing women who had "been there" in life. Since I was recently widowed, and had two children to raise, these late afternoon sessions were just what the doctor ordered. A lot of woman-to-woman advice was dispensed there, including one puzzling admonition from Virginia: "Don't ever remarry when you are feeling down." And this brings me to Victor.

Victor was a small, dark man with a chiseled face that cried out to be in a Dickens novel. I knew he would be an unforgettable character the day I met him. He'd been successful in business, and in his retirement years allowed himself the luxury of criticizing the way those who came after him comported themselves. No one seemed to measure up to Victor's standards. Perhaps that's what Virginia meant when she spoke of not marrying when you are down; Victor was probably not the cheeriest of mates, yet he was a most interesting character.

Victor was also intensely frugal. He hardly ever paid full freight for anything, and was quite adept at talking vendors down from their original prices. One day I drove him over to a shop where we would both have our lawn mowers serviced. As we were leaving, he took the repair man aside and I heard him say, "Now I want you to cut her bill down by a substantial margin because this young woman is a poor minister's widow." It was an embarrassing moment for me but another triumph for Victor. And sure enough, when the bill came, I only had to pay "the widow's mite."

When Victor's health began to fail he would often appear at my door saying he was like Oliver Wendell Holmes' "The Last Leaf," and would quote stanzas from memory. Soon, on a Sunday afternoon after his death, a few of us were sitting in a small church chapel, waiting for the minister to arrive. After twenty-five minutes, I left to find a phone to call him. It was obvious from his tone that he had simply forgotten all about conducting this funeral service. He promised to be right down, and shortly he came through the door looking very calm and in command of the situation. Suddenly he glanced up from the lectern and asked whether Joann Duncanson would please step out into the hall. What he needed to know from me was very basic: the name of the deceased. Once I told him, we both re-entered the chapel and I thought that was it. But no. Again he motioned me outside the chapel. "Which of those three white-haired ladies is his wife?" I pointed Virginia out to him and Victor finally had his funeral.

We had some good times back on Ruthellen Road, and I couldn't have asked for better neighbors—even Victor. In some ways he turned out to be the most fascinating of all. And I'm willing to bet that had he known about that funeral mixup, he'd have insisted on a discount.

JSD

FINDING THE LOST TRIBES

Once upon a time—in biblical days—there were twelve Hebrew tribes, each named after a son of Jacob: Reuben, Simeon, Levi, Judah, Issachar, Zebulun, Joseph, Benjamin, Dan, Naphtali, Gad, and Asher. After a series of lost wars and consequent dispersals and assimilations, ten of the tribes vanished from the scene. Only two were left in historical awareness: Judah and Issachar. The specific fates of the ten lost tribes remain a mystery to this day.

Romantic that I am, I have long been on the lookout for signs of these lost tribes. So, recently, while watching a Democrat convention, my interest was sparked when the keynote speaker, Barak Obama, was introduced and a commentator remarked that "barak" meant "blessing" in the language of Kenya, the land of Mr. Obama's father.

Well, it just so happens that in Hebrew, "barookh"* means "blessed" and many Hebrew prayers begin with that word. Couldn't this mean that the Kenyans are one of the lost tribes?

All this reminded me of another coincidence. In the Hawaiian language, "kahana" means "priest." Well, guess what? In Hebrew, "cohen" means "priest;" so allowing for the nature of the two languages, "kahana" and "cohen" are obviously the same word.

And that's not all there is to this Hawaiian-Hebrew connection. In Hawaiian, "aloha" is generally translated in the same way as is the Hebrew "shalom:" "Hello, goodbye, peace." When we consider that the Hawaiian language does not have an "s," then "aloha" is easily seen as a close approximation of "shalom." These words—priest and

* "kh" is the gutteral sound between "h" and "k." Often, "ch" is used instead of "kh"—but, alas, too many people then mispronounce the "ch" as the "ch" sound in "church."

hello/goodbye/peace—are not trivial concepts; they are key concepts for the cultures involved. So as far as I'm concerned, I've just found a second lost tribe—the Hawaiians!

Now, this search for the lost tribes needn't be limited to language concurrences. For instance, have you ever noticed the similarity between ravioli and kreplakh, and that between won-ton and kreplakh? So, given these culinary tie-ins, are not the Italians and Chinese also lost tribes?

And while we are at it, one of my favorite professors at the University of Hawaii, Doug Yamamura, looked to be an absolute clone of my beloved "Uncle" Louis Grossman. So there you have it—the Japanese must be a lost tribe, too.

Just as I suspected—the whole world *is* Jewish, after all!

Note: I just heard on the BBC that an apparent lost tribe of Jews has been discovered in north India, having been there since the 8th century. (I am not joking here.) Perhaps you, dear reader, have come across other clues as to the fate of those lost tribes. I would love to hear of them. It would be gratifying to know that we are all indeed brothers and sisters.

Aloha, khavayrim! (Peace, friends!)

FS

THE SEA

If the sea is so vast—
so wondrously endless
with its fathoms and leagues,
its miles of rolling tides—
why then do you suppose
it was given
such
a
tiny
name
?

JSD

TRADE WINDS GONE HAYWIRE

The time: Tuesday, November 16th—7:30 AM.
The place: An oceanside resort on the island of Aruba.

Riiiiiiing! Riiiiiiing!

I open my eyes and make a quick decision that the sound was coming from the telephone. "Hello," I mumble.

"Good morning," says a voice on the other end of the line, "we are moving you. Please have your luggage outside your door in 25 minutes."

"Is it because of the rain?" I ask. I vaguely remembered that despite the roar of the noisy air conditioner, I did hear some rain in the night.

"Yes," says she, and hangs up.

After putting the phone down I glanced at the floor. Her "yes" was an understatement; water was already seeping into the room from under the sliding glass door.

Now, let me go back and set the scene for you.

One brisk fall day, Fred and I decided that a trip to a sunny clime just before the holiday crazies set in would be just the thing we needed. Several friends recommended the island of Aruba which is Dutch owned, located just 17 miles north of Venezuela, has temperatures that hardly ever deviate from the 82-86 degree range, gentle trade winds, and boasts of never having much more than a dozen inches of rain a year. This, combined with the fact that their slogan is "One happy island!" made it hard to resist. We called the travel agent and signed up.

Later, we viewed a promotional video of Aruba, and sure enough, they again pointed to their perfect weather, and said whatever rain did fall, fell in November. That should have been a clue right there, but we still said we'd go. We figured it would probably rain just at night—so what's the problem? Besides, there was one more claim to fame as far as Aruba is concerned—even though located in the Caribbean, it is out of the hurricane belt. A real plus, as far as we were concerned.

When we got to the airport on the 13th (that should have been another clue), we found over 300 other sun-seeking souls in line at the check-in counter, some already dressed for Caribbean weather. We, on the other hand, went as skeptical New Englanders, lugging jackets and raincoats, and in the suitcases—just in case—two umbrellas!

The moment we touched down at the hot, steamy airport we knew we were woefully overdressed. We rolled the raincoats up into tight balls, and prayed that the suitcases wouldn't suddenly spring open, exposing those umbrellas.

Shunning the towering high-rise hotels, we opted for a low-rise one with units as close to the water as you can get. At the front desk we discovered that though they speak a bit of our language, we didn't understand a word of theirs. At the end of it all, however, we had somehow managed to give them credit card information, sign in, get the key to the room safe (in case we won big in the casino), and the room keys. (This should have been another clue—Room 1313.)

Just outside my door it looked like a scene from *South Pacific*—I expected someone to break into a chorus of "Some Enchanted Evening" any moment; turquoise blue water, swaying palm trees, white sandy beaches as far as the eye could see. And the distance from Room 1313 to the sea wall was no more than 25 feet. I could get to like this place.

Then there was the food. At this resort, you have the option of purchasing an all-inclusive package so that all your food and drinks are included. Indulgence was the name of the game here. Guests of all sizes, shapes, and nationalities lined up daily to help themselves to some incredible gastronomical offerings.

As you probably have guessed, the Caribbean islands are not without creeping and crawling things. How about iguanas, for instance? All sizes of this lizard family dart in and out of bushes and across paths with amazing speed and regularity in Aruba. It was not uncommon to be having lunch on the outdoor terrace when a green iguana, more than 2 feet in length including tail, would amble by, looking for a handout of lettuce. After a while I became less fearful and more interested in these strange creatures, though it did strike me that with their appetite for green lettuce, that they could have been cavorting about in the huge salad bowl before dinner and no one would have been able to spot them. (I didn't eat lettuce once on the entire trip.)

Then there are some smaller crawling things. On the second day there I noticed a line of tiny ant-like critters scurrying across the counter next to the bathroom sink. The place was kept spotless, so I couldn't imagine what was attracting them. Later that day I found out. I have a small tin box in which I keep a few aspirin for occasional headaches, and some estrogen tablets for hormone replacement therapy. When I opened that box I found out the hard way what was attracting those mini-ants! There had to be *hundreds* of them jammed in there, happily swarming all over those tablets. I'm not sure which ones they were going for, but what I do know is that either they'll never have to worry about headaches, or the ant population in Aruba will take a significant jump this year.

So anyway, here we were enjoying the sun, water, food—yes, and even the little critters—when suddenly on the morning of the 16th that phone call came. "Good morning—we are moving you...."

The ensuing frantic packing scene was reminiscent of the Keystone Cops' silent movie days, only on *fast forward.* This procedure was hastened by what I saw when I pulled back the drapes of the room. There on the patio, jammed up against the sliding glass door, was piled sand, rocks, coral, broken palm branches, and all manner of patio furniture. Even more frightening was the fact that the sea level was even with the sea wall and flowing steadily toward Room 1313. This was no ordinary rainstorm, this was Hurricane

Lenny, gracing us right there in Aruba where they hardly ever have rain and NEVER have hurricanes!

We knew we were being evacuated—but to where? We had visions of sleeping on a school gymnasium floor for days. (I began to wonder whether there'd be any iguanas bunking out there too.) Luckily, they put us in an upscale condominium complex just across the street, complete with fully equipped kitchen, dining and living rooms, Jacuzzis, three patios, and a pool. It turned out to be a bonus, thanks to Lenny.

Unfortunately, Lenny was not so kind to the island of Aruba or the other harder hit islands in the Caribbean. The beaches in front of Room 1313 and beyond were all torn up, trees uprooted, boats smashed. The earth beneath the tiles of the dining terrace was swept away—bulldozers and backhoes were still hard at work the day we left for home.

This surely wasn't what Fred and I had in mind when we signed up for a peaceful pre-holiday vacation. Little did we know this quiet little paradise would provide such excitement. As we were leaving the island, putting our holiday behind us, Her Royal Majesty Queen Beatrix of the Netherlands was just arriving. We hoped she didn't get to see the typo on Page One of the "Aruba Today" newspaper which stated, "...although her stay will be very short, her itinerary is very *impertinent*." Oh, and for heaven's sake, let's hope she keeps her aspirin and hormones in an airtight container. Those little crawling things can take just so much excitement in one year!

JSD

Note: *Though our Hurricane Lenny experience brought with it some danger, we, of course, recognize that it pales in comparison to the devastating 2004 Indian Ocean tsunami. We are humbled by the pain and courage of the tsunami survivors.... And now there is Hurricane Katrina with its brave victims.*

FS and JSD

SPECK-TACULAR: EXPLODING THE BIG-BANG THEORY

Most of us are so awed by science and mathematics that a scientist or mathematician can state just about any-thing—no matter how absurd—and we will tend to agree with the claim. This is especially so if the vast majority of other scientists/mathematicians concur with the claim. If it weren't so frightening, this would be amusing to the nth degree.

One of the most absurd such claims is that the "Big-Bang" theory explains the origin of the universe. Simply put, it asserts that one extremely small speck of concentrat-ed matter exploded and the whole blasted universe came out of it. We are talking about a universe with myriad galaxies and myriad stars within each galaxy—some stars so dense, so concentrated in matter, that light cannot escape from them—the "black holes." (Recently a new theory was put forth claiming that, aha!, light *can* escape—but the *den-sity* of the black holes remains undisputed.)

The funny thing is that most people I have come across seem to swallow the Big-Bang theory hook, line, and sinker. (So many hungry fish. Hungry for explanations, we must understand—it is necessary for mental balance. So when we are told by an authority that such and such is so, we are eager to accept it.)

But just a moment. Let us consider the situation using our natural ability to think—never mind the complexities and confusions of mathematics and science. Reason. Common sense. Let us not desert these friends of the human mind.

I ask you—can a multitude of stars, some of which are as dense as black holes, emanate from one *infinitesimal* speck no matter how dense, how compact that speck may be? Let *us* not be dense!

Using your own good sense, can you imagine even one black hole star coming out of one speck? Now, many of us have seen ten, twenty, thirty clowns pour out of an automobile at a circus. Quite a surprise, yet believable. But would you believe ads which promised that *millions* of clowns would topple out of one car?

The humor of the Big-Bang theory claiming to explain the origin of the universe does not end there. How in the world did that mighty speck come to be? Before that, how did the space within which that speck was residing come to be? And since we are exploring the matter with our open, unfettered minds, how did time begin?

For the most part, their mathematics just *describe* their *theory* and put numbers on concepts. Elegant mathematics can be quite impressive—but that does not make the theory true. It is a theory—unproven. Think freely, friends, with your natural intelligence. It is all quite amazing, is it not?

Now I do not claim to have the answer to the origin of the universe, and I have enough good sense and humility to *admit* that I do not know. But there must be an explanation somewhere, somehow, sometime. As far as I'm concerned, the exalted Big-Bang theory is not it!

Of course, if the proponents of the theory were to emphasize that—aha!—their founding speck must have been a *miraculous* speck indeed—then that "explains" everything. It just might be that these avowed scientists are in effect telling us that the speck——is *God.*

FS

ENCORE

LIFE'S LITTLE LAUGH

Perhaps it is no joke, this growing old.
And memories of stellar plays
on the ballfields of your youth hold
meager solace for these latter days
as you roll you out of bed
in obeissance to arthritic hips,
and you walk with feet of lead
and the ragged carpet trips
you—but you do retain your balance
for you have not given in,
and you bless your several talents
which keep you in the spin
of life, and the morning tai chi calms
the spirit and keeps the bod in tone
and your back and legs and arms
work together, not alone—
and you smile at your own rhyming
and the rather jagged timing.

But you've *earned* a bit o' joking
when you're getting close to croaking.

                                        FS

FRED SAMUELS bravely began writing poetry at age eleven. Later, as a professor of sociology, he incorporated poetry into his courses at the University of New Hampshire. His book, *Intense Experience: Social Psychology through Poetry*, is an effective teaching tool.

Meanwhile, the older he gets, the more he appreciates the need for humor, to be able to smile and to help others smile. Having found a gifted partner in such crime (Joann), you, dear reader, are now the beneficiary.

Fred is a long-time, active member of the Poetry Society of New Hampshire.

Photograph by Joyce Whiting.

JOANN SNOW DUNCANSON began her writing career as a humorous verse editor for Rust Craft Greeting Card Co. in Boston, and subsequently became a newspaper columnist—for the last 16 years with the Peterborough Transcript (Peterborough, NH). She is a past winner of the Columnist of the Year Award, given by the NH Press Association and is the author of the book, *Who Gets the Yellow Bananas?*

Joann is also known for her musical performances on the life and works of both Emily Dickinson and Isles of Shoals poet, Celia Thaxter, and her humorous talks on the foibles of everyday life.

Photograph by Jean Webster.